VISUAL QUICKSTART GUIDE

MICROSOFT OFFICE
Access 2003

FOR WINDOWS

Steve Schwartz

 Peachpit Press

Visual QuickStart Guide
Microsoft Office Access 2003 for Windows
Steve Schwartz

Peachpit Press
1249 Eighth Street
Berkeley, CA 94710
510/524-2178
800/283-9444
510/524-2221 (fax)

Find us on the World Wide Web at: http://www.peachpit.com
To report errors, please send a note to errata@peachpit.com
Peachpit Press is a division of Pearson Education

Copyright © 2004 by Steve Schwartz

Editor: Suki Gear
Production Coordinator: Gloria Márquez
Copy Editor: Ben Greensfelder
Technical Editor: Charles Seiter
Compositor: Steve Schwartz
Indexer: Beth Palmer
Cover Design: Peachpit Press
Cover Production: George Mattingly

Some text in Chapter 11 was derived from *Access 2000 for Windows: Visual QuickStart Guide,* by Deborah S. Ray and Eric J. Ray.

Notice of Rights

Notice of Liability

Trademarks

ISBN 0-321-19393-8

9 8 7 6 5 4

Printed and bound in the United States of America

TABLE OF CONTENTS

INTRODUCTION

Welcome to the *Microsoft Office Access 2003 for Windows: Visual QuickStart Guide.* This book is a visual, step-by-step guide to Access, a component of the Microsoft Office 2003 suite.

Access and you

Let's try a little mind reading. Since this book is in your hands, there are two likely scenarios that may have prompted you to buy it:

◆ Someone in your organization said: "Hey, *<your name here>*. The company databases are all in Microsoft Office Access. You'll have to learn how to use it."

◆ As an owner of Office, you've noticed that it includes Access, a database program. Whether or not you've used a database before, you've probably heard that they can be useful for organizing and viewing data. Might as well learn to use it, right?

In either case, you launched Access and plunged ahead. However, you soon made two important discoveries. First, when you reached for the manual, you found that there *wasn't* one—not even a PDF version on the CD. (Microsoft has conducted user surveys that revealed few people ever opened a manual, making it permissible to eliminate them.)

Second, when you tried to create your own database—even a very basic one—you found that simple activities in Access are often neither simple nor obvious.

To its credit, Access includes a Help system and a set of browser-based tutorials. While these learning aids will give you a smattering of information, they're more likely to confuse you than give you a grounding in the program.

An analogous situation is that of taking a car trip through Cambridge, MA. As you drive, you'll note that the corner street signs are very different from ones you've seen elsewhere. Most display only the cross street name—seldom showing the name of the street you're on. When I asked a local why this was so, he explained: "If you're from here, you already *know* what street you're on." I think the expectation is the same for Access users. If you're using the program, the assumption is that you already know how.

How this book can help you

My assumption, however, is that you *don't* know how. The purpose of this book is to help you understand how Access works, enabling you to enter and edit data in other people's databases as well as to create usable databases of your own. While this book will not transform you into a professional Access developer, it will point you in the right direction.

If you've never read a Visual QuickStart Guide, you'll note that this book has some distinctive differences from other computer books. First, each chapter is written as a self-contained unit. For example, if you just want to learn about printing, you can turn directly to the chapter on that topic. Thus, although you *can* read the book in chapter order, there's no requirement that you do so.

Second, chapters laid out in a consistent format—a format created by the series designers to make information as easy to digest as possible. Every page is laid out as two columns. The outer column holds the text and the inner column contains illustrative screen shots (which are referred to by number in the text). Major headings always begin at the top of a column, enabling you to quickly see where you should start reading to learn about a program feature. Minor headings can appear anywhere, but are always subtopics of the major heading that precedes them.

About the author

Steve Schwartz has been a computer industry writer since the days of the early micros. He's used scores of database programs and is the author of the bestselling *FileMaker Pro Bible* (Wiley). He has written for dozens of computer magazines and is the author of more than 50 computer and game books, including these Visual QuickStarts: *Picture It! 7, Microsoft Office v. X, CorelDRAW 10* and *11, Entourage 2001, Internet Explorer 3* and *5,* and *Quicken 6.*

Steve has a Ph.D. in psychology and lives with his sons and pets in the fictional town of Lizard Spit, Arizona. He can be reached via his official Web site at www.siliconwasteland.com.

1

DATABASE CONCEPTS

Even if Access is the first database program you've ever used, there's no need to worry. In this chapter, you'll learn the fundamental concepts needed to use *any* database program. Once you understand the terminology, Access and other database programs will be less intimidating to you.

This chapter discusses databases in general terms. In Chapter 2, you'll learn specifically how Access works. (Note that if you've previously used another database program, skimming this chapter will probably suffice.)

Databases All Around You

At its simplest, a *database* is an organized collection of information. Receipts stuffed in an envelope are certainly information, but they need to be organized in a consistent manner to be considered a database.

Not all databases are computer based; many are paper only. A phone book is an example of a paper database. It contains a name, address, and telephone number for every listed individual and business (**Figure 1.1**). Organization is imposed on the data in two ways. First, the specific bits of information presented for each entry are standardized. Second, every entry is alphabetized by last name or company name. Other examples of paper databases include vendor and employee records stored in the file cabinets of most businesses, as well as the recipes that you or a relative painstakingly transcribed onto index cards.

Unfortunately, paper-based databases have limitations. Correcting errors can be cumbersome or even impossible. An incorrect number in a phone book, for instance, will remain incorrect until the next printing. And if you want to use the data for another purpose, it often requires retyping and manual sorting.

As we progress from paper to electronic databases, capabilities and flexibility improve. For example, a handheld organizer or PDA (personal digital assistant) typically includes an address book component that you can use to enter contact information and search for specific people. This is an example of a single-purpose database application for managing personal and business contacts. While it's reasonably useful, such a database may not let you print a phone directory, sort by anything other than last name or company, be extended by adding other bits of information (such as notes or an additional phone number), or be modified to record an entirely different type of data (such as the holdings of your extensive wine collection).

Name or business   *Address*   *Phone*

Schwartz Steven 1854 Jones Dr **453-7812**

Figure 1.1 Every listing in a phone book contains the same basic elements presented in the same order. Explicit rules for creating the listings give the phone book consistency.

Figure 1.2 Address Book is a special-purpose, Windows database application that you can use to manage contact information.

The Windows Address Book (**Figure 1.2**) is more advanced than a PDA or handheld address book. Because Address Book is computer based, you can sort the entries by name, email address, business phone, or home phone, as well as print the contact information in several useful, preset formats.

Address Book is actually a dedicated database program. What distinguishes it from a database that you might create in an application such as Microsoft Access is that it is not customizable. That is, you can only record the kinds of information it is already designed to collect, you can't perform calculations, and you're restricted to using the provided forms for recording, viewing, and printing your data.

Customizability is the hallmark of most computer database programs. Using one to create your own databases, you can do any of the following:

- You decide what pieces of information to collect. If you later need to record additional types of data, you can freely modify the database to do so.

- You can create custom forms on which to record and view the data. Each form need only show the specific data that is relevant to the form. For example, in an employee database, you might have one form for recording general background data and another on which to record only salary history and quarterly review notes.

- When viewing the database, you can sort by any piece of information (such as Last Name) or by several pieces of information (such as Zip Code within City). You can also view subsets of data, such as only the employees with children under the age of 5.

- You can perform calculations, such as totaling the items purchased by each person (as part of an invoice) or totaling all of the invoices across the entire database.

Parts of a Database

Databases maintain consistency by organizing data into fields and records. A *field* is a named entity designed to record a single piece of data of a particular type. For example, a database might contain Last Name, Salary, and Hire Date fields, defined to be a Text, a Number, and a Date field, respectively.

Available *field types* are specific to the database program you're using. The main purpose of field types is to restrict the kinds of data that can be entered in a given field. For example, a Number field might only allow you to enter a string composed of the digits 0–9, an optional decimal point (.), and an optional minus (-) sign. Other characters, such as letters or punctuation marks, would result in an invalid entry.

A *record* is the collective data (all fields) recorded for one person or thing in the database. As an example, a CD collection database (**Table 1.1**) might have separate fields for Artist, Title, Recording Date, and Music Category. The information gathered in the fields for each CD would constitute a record. From top to bottom, Table 1.1 contains four records, each one a separate row in the table.

✔ Tips

■ Looking at Table 1.1, you might note that it resembles a spreadsheet (like you create in Excel). In fact, a spreadsheet can easily double as a database. Each row would represent a record, and each column would be a field (**Figure 1.3**).

■ When defining fields, it's best to make them as discrete as possible. For instance, while you might be tempted to create a Name field to record each person's full name, it's usually better to create separate First Name and Last Name fields. Doing so gives you greater flexibility when entering data, searching for data subsets or specific records, and presenting the data in reports.

ID field   Artist field   Title field

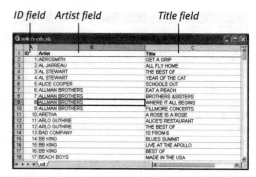

Figure 1.3 You can create rudimentary databases in a spreadsheet program. This simple CD database has three columns that correspond to database fields: ID, Artist, and Title.

Table 1.1

Records from a CD Collection Database

ARTIST	TITLE	DATE	CATEGORY
Frank Zappa	Zoot Allures	1976	Rock
Robert Cray	Strong Persuader	1986	Blues
Big Bad Voodoo Daddy	Big Bad Voodoo...	1998	Swing
Psykosonik	Psykosonik	1997	Techno

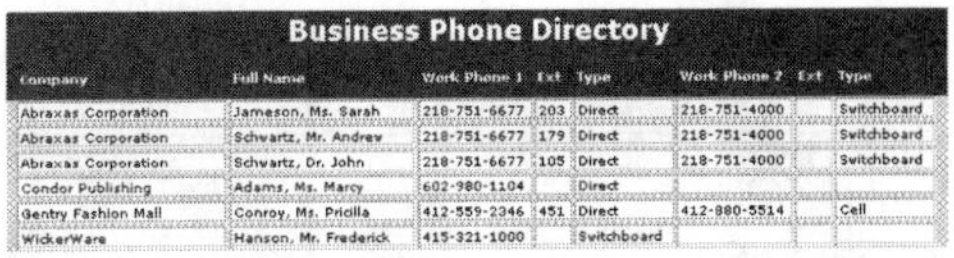

Business Phone Directory

Company	Full Name	Work Phone 1	Ext	Type	Work Phone 2	Ext	Type
Abraxas Corporation	Jameson, Ms. Sarah	218-751-6677	203	Direct	218-751-4000		Switchboard
Abraxas Corporation	Schwartz, Mr. Andrew	218-751-6677	179	Direct	218-751-4000		Switchboard
Abraxas Corporation	Schwartz, Dr. John	218-751-6677	105	Direct	218-751-4000		Switchboard
Condor Publishing	Adams, Ms. Marcy	602-980-1104		Direct			
Gentry Fashion Mall	Conroy, Ms. Pricilla	412-559-2346	451	Direct	412-880-5514		Cell
WickerWare	Hanson, Mr. Frederick	415-321-1000		Switchboard			

Figure 1.4 To make it easier to find the desired person, this phone directory report was prepared by sorting on three fields: Company, Last Name, and First Name.

Sorting Records

Unless you're working with a static database, the order in which you enter records will probably have no special meaning. Luckily, all database programs have a sort capability that enables you to modify the order in which records are displayed. In most programs, sorts can be conducted based on the contents of a single field or multiple fields. Each sort can be in ascending or descending order.

For example, in an address book database, you might want to sort by Last Name, Company Name, or Zip Code—depending on your current need. While useful, sorting by a single field can result in many instances in which multiple records have the same data in the sort field. Sorting by Last Name, for instance, might result in a list of 72 Johnsons—in no useful order. To break these ties and present the data in a more useful fashion, you can add additional sort fields (**Figure 1.4**). Performing an ascending sort by both Last Name *and* First Name will result in the 72 Johnsons being listed together, but alphabetized by first names.

✔ Tips

- In addition to sorting while viewing or making changes to your database, sorting plays an equally important role in reports. For example, when sorting by salesperson as part of a report, advanced databases will group relevant sales together, making it possible to generate subtotals for each salesperson.
- Advanced database programs let you specify fields that you want to be automatically tracked and sorted as you make changes to the database. The term for this process is *indexing*. Important fields that you regularly sort by or include in searches are the best candidates for indexing, since it greatly improves the speed of both operations.

Selecting Records

While it's convenient to have all the data from a given database at your disposal, there will be many times when you'll want to see only one specific record or a particular subset of the data. Here are a few examples:

◆ There's a fresh chicken in your refrigerator. You open your recipe database and select only the recipes that list *chicken* in the Main Ingredient field.

◆ It's time to write the monthly bonus checks for your sales force. Since bonuses are paid only to those who met their quota, you select only those records.

◆ Your company wants to do a local mass mailing to advertise an upcoming sale. Rather than paying for printing and mailing flyers to everyone in town, you refer to your customer database. After selecting only your active customers within a specific range of zip codes, you produce the desired set of mailing labels.

Selecting records is generally done by issuing a Search or Find command and then specifying one or more selection criteria (**Figure 1.5**). Searches can be based on a single criterion (invoices over $500), multiple criteria (contacts from Boston whose birthdays are in May), or either of multiple criteria (from New Hampshire *or* from New York).

Selecting subsets of data can be useful when you're browsing through records, performing calculations over the subset, or generating reports. You can also use a search to identify a group of records on which to perform another operation, such as deleting inactive customers or applying an across-the-board price increase. You can also use the search feature to find a *specific* record, as you might do in order to locate Tasha Simpson's phone number or her invoice #24761.

Search criterion

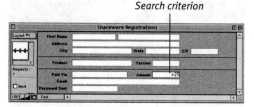

Figure 1.5 In FileMaker Pro, you can type search criteria in any data layout. This example will find all sales of more than $25.

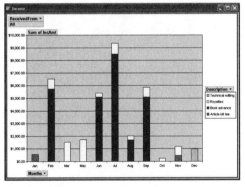

Detail Report by Category

Date	Description	Income	Expense
10/29	Tires		174.32
10/30	Oil change		22.81
10/31	Mileage (239)		77.68
11/30	Mileage (131)		42.58
12/31	Mileage (140)		45.50
			$1,854.65
	Commissions and fees		
1/10	Auction fees		7.91
3/11	Auction fees		20.36
4/12	Auction fees		41.65
5/15	Auction fees		9.86
6/12	Auction fees		3.35
9/7	Auction fees		8.45
11/5	Auction fees		30.31
11/10	Auction fees		5.55
12/17	Domain registration		12.70
			$140.14
	Deprec. and sect. 179		
5/27	Epson inkjet		107.87
8/14	Computer		848.96
			$956.83

Figure 1.6 In this portion of a report, expenses are presented in date order within each expense category. A subtotal is displayed for each category.

Figure 1.7 This PivotChart (an interactive graph created in Microsoft Access) shows monthly income by income type.

Generating Reports

Databases are excellent tools for creating detailed reports. Though browsing through individual records can be useful, it doesn't hold a candle to seeing your data in a nicely organized report.

A *report* is an onscreen or printed arrangement of all or a subset of your data in a particular sort order (**Figure 1.6**). A report may include calculations, such as group subtotals (sales per item type, for example) and grand totals.

Reports enable you to use the data for a variety of purposes. For example, a company sales database might be used to create any of the following reports:

◆ A customer or salesperson phone directory

◆ Mailing labels for all or a subset of customers

◆ Sales totals by region or period of time (months, quarters, or years)

◆ A further breakdown of sales by salesperson, item color, item category, or any other classifying characteristic

◆ A list of all customers with past due accounts, enabling you to generate custom dunning letters and mailing labels

The key is that every database can have as few or as many reports as you wish. Unlike Address Book (which restricts you to a handful of preset reports), database programs enable you to create a new report whenever the need arises. You can also format the data in whatever manner you like. You can generally use multiple fonts, font styles and sizes, and even add graphics, such as a company logo. Some database programs even let you create charts and graphs based on the data, such as income received by type (**Figure 1.7**).

Automating Databases

Most database applications offer some way to automate actions. They often include a macro recorder or a scripting language. If there's a report that you print at the end of every month, for example, you can specify all the preparatory steps so that the report can be created at the click of a button or by choosing its name from a menu. The macro or script might select only the records needed for the report, sort them in a particular order, specify a form or layout on which to display the results, and then send the resulting report to your printer. Macros or scripts enable you to perform both simple and complex actions, such as switching from the current data layout to a different one; automating a backup, import, or export procedure; or providing an options menu that helps users navigate your database (**Figure 1.8**).

Macro and scripting languages vary widely from one program to the next. At the low end are simple macro recorders that watch your actions and then store them for later playback. At the other extreme, working with a high-end scripting facility may require you to learn a programming or scripting language, such as Visual Basic. In general, the more complex the scripting language, the greater the flexibility you'll have in performing precisely the actions you want.

Recording or scripting even simple actions can save you an extraordinary amount of time compared to executing them manually whenever they're needed. A carefully constructed macro or script also ensures that the action is performed correctly and consistently each time—whether you run it yourself or a temp is asked to execute it.

Open the help file — Help buttons — Help file

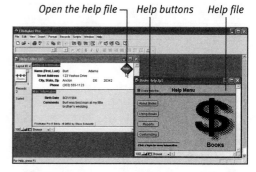

Figure 1.8 When you associate a script with a button, a database can perform an action when the button is clicked. The buttons shown here open the help file and help the user navigate within it.

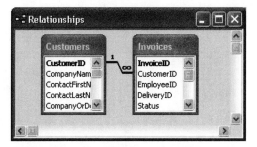

Figure 1.9 Access graphically depicts relationships. In this one-to-many relationship (linked by the CustomerID field), a record in the Customers table can have many possible matching records in the Invoices table.

Flat File and Relational Databases

Not all databases and database applications are alike. There are two general types: flat file and relational. While all database programs are capable of creating flat file databases, only the more advanced applications (such as Access) support relational databases.

A *flat file database* contains all of its fields and data in a single file or data table. While this makes flat file databases incredibly easy to construct and understand, it can result in extensive data duplication. For example, consider an invoice database that's used to record customer sales. Assuming that you may make multiple sales to a customer, the database will be required to store the customer's address in each of his or her invoice records—dramatically increasing the size of the file.

Properly constructed *relational databases,* on the other hand, can avoid much of the unnecessary data duplication. A relational database contains additional files or tables that are linked to each other by matching fields. In the invoice example, you might have two database files or tables: one that contains only the data relevant to the invoice (such as the date and items ordered) and a second that contains only customer address information. By including a Customer ID number in both files or tables, the invoice layout can automatically reference correct address information for each invoice (**Figure 1.9**).

In this simple example, there is a one-to-many relationship (the most common type). For every customer in the addresses file/table, there are potentially many invoices. Other relationship types include one-to-one and many-to-many. The specific types supported vary from one database program to the next.

There are several important advantages of separating the address information from the actual invoices (and these advantages apply to *all* relational databases):

♦ Address data only has to be entered once per customer—regardless of the number of invoices generated for that customer.

♦ In each new invoice, the customer address will automatically be referenced and appear on the invoice form. You don't need to enter anything other than the appropriate Customer ID number.

♦ Referencing address data requires considerably less disk space than copying or retyping it for every invoice (as you'd need to do in a flat file database). This is also much faster than retyping the data.

♦ If a customer's address changes, you only have to make the correction in one place— the customer's Address record. Matching invoices can automatically display the new address.

In case you're wondering why all databases that could benefit from it aren't relational, there's one big reason. Conceptually, relational databases are more difficult to plan and set up than flat file databases. And the necessary relationships are often more numerous and complex than in my simple example. In an accounting database, for example, there might easily be dozens of linked files/tables, as well as a maze of relationships to be defined.

✔ Tip

■ Even if a relational database would be more parsimonious in a given instance, no database program will *require* you to constuct one. If you don't feel comfortable designing a relational solution, you can still create a flat file solution.

An Overview of Access

In Chapter 1, you learned basic database concepts. This chapter, on the other hand, is specific to Access (now called *Microsoft Office Access*).

Some caveats are in order. Unless you've previously used another high-end table-based database, you'll find Access to be a difficult program to learn and use. Unlike the other main applications in Microsoft Office (Word, Excel, PowerPoint, and Outlook), Access is not a program that is immediately obvious and understandable.

Before starting this book, I leafed through half a dozen elementary books on Access and discovered a commonality among them. Not one provided a comprehensive overview of the program or its terminology. Thus, my intent in this chapter is to start you off right by showing you *The Big Picture*—how Access works, how its many components fit together, and how you will eventually use them to create, modify, and enter data in databases. Once you see how the pieces of this software puzzle fit together, it is my hope that the more specific material presented in later chapters won't confuse you.

Key Concepts and Features

The following sections will help familiarize you with Access' basic concepts and features.

Tables and datasheets

Regardless of the method used to create an Access database, the immediate result is at least one table. A *table* is a repository for data. The expression of a table is called a *datasheet*, a worksheet-like arrangement of rows and columns (**Figure 2.1**). Each row is a single record and each column is a single field.

If you don't mind their simple format, you can use datasheets to perform all common database activities, such as adding, deleting, and editing records; sorting; and filtering the data to display only records that meet your criteria. Adding and deleting fields, as well as changing a field's data type, are also done in the datasheet.

Related tables

Because Access is a relational database, each table generally stores data on only one topic, such as address information, delivery services, or catalog items. To enable you to relate tables to one another, you create a primary key field for each table.

A *primary key field* is one that contains a unique number for every record. The number can be assigned by Access whenever a new record is created. Or if you have an existing unique numbering system, such as part numbers or Social Security numbers, you can make that field the primary key.

Relationships are graphically created and managed in the Relationships window (**Figure 2.2**). A relationship is defined by a pair of matching fields in two tables. In the main table, the field is the primary key. In the other table, it's an ordinary field referred to as a *foreign key*. The names of the matching fields are unimportant. However, both fields must contain the same type of data.

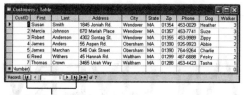

Navigation controls

Figure 2.1 This is a typical datasheet. Note the controls for navigating among records.

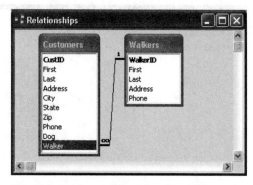

Figure 2.2 In this two-table dog walker database, the relationship is the match between the Walker and WalkerID fields. Every customer has one dog walker, and every walker can have multiple customers.

Databases and Projects

In addition to the databases discussed in this book, you can also create Access projects. A *project* provides a means of interacting with data tables stored on a Microsoft SQL (Structured Query Language) server. Projects are not discussed in this book.

Open the Customers form

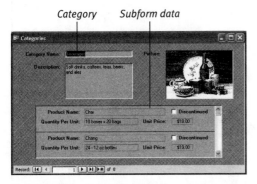

Figure 2.3 This simple form is designed to gather basic employee data. Note that unlike datasheets, forms can contain special items, such as buttons and graphics.

Category   Subform data

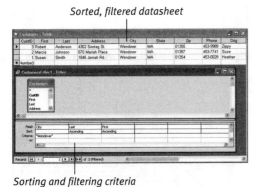

Figure 2.4 This subform displays all products for the selected category.

Sorted, filtered datasheet

Sorting and filtering criteria

Figure 2.5 You can create an Advanced Filter/Sort that includes filtering criteria and sort instructions. In this example, only records with Wendover as the City are displayed, sorted by the Last and First fields.

Custom forms

While you can certainly perform data entry chores using datasheets, things can occasionally get messy—particularly when a database involves many tables. To enter an order for a new customer, for example, you might have to enter data in several datasheets.

To make data entry easier, Access lets you create *forms* (**Figure 2.3**): layouts that show only the fields for which you want to gather data, arranged in an attractive manner. Forms can also display data from related tables. While the form backgrounds that Access provides vary from boring to ugly, you can use your own patterns or pictures, if you prefer.

Forms can also include subforms. A *subform* shows related data from another table or query. For example, the Northwind sample database has a Categories form that uses a subform to show all products for a given category (**Figure 2.4**). The subform data is taken from the Products table.

Sorting, filters, and queries

By default, datasheets and forms display all records in their normal sort order; that is, arranged in order of the primary key field. Because this isn't always the way you'd like to view the data, you can use Access features to change the sort order or display only a subset of records (**Figure 2.5**).

You can sort by one or several fields in ascending or descending order. When sorting by multiple fields, you specify the most important field first. For example, you might sort an address table on City, Last Name, and First Name fields.

To specify a data subset to view, you can apply a *filter* (showing only records that contain CA in the State field, for example) or construct a complex *query* containing many criteria. Sort and filtering instruction are specific to the database object for which they were created.

Reports

Access reports present and summarize data. Rather than viewing records one at a time or in a scrolling list as you'd do with forms or datasheets, you can display all of your data (or a selected subset) in an easy to comprehend fashion (**Figure 2.6**). You can also specify one or multiple sort fields, as well as grouping fields. The latter enable you to automatically split the data into convenient groups, such as months (examining purchases over the current year, for example) or sales regions.

PivotTables and PivotCharts

Access has some data analysis features not commonly found in database software. First, using Microsoft Graph (an integrated component of Office), you can create colorful graphs and charts from selected data. Second, you can also generate interactive tables (PivotTables) and charts (PivotCharts). Based on a statistical function known as a crosstab, PivotTables (**Figure 2.7**) and PivotCharts allow you to view one field broken down by another. For example, you could create a PivotTable or PivotChart to show the breakdown of employee rank by sex. You can also add grouping levels for more detailed breakdowns.

Data access pages

Any database can be opened for use by one person *(exclusive mode)* or multiple users on a network *(shared mode)*. You can also post a database on the Internet or a company intranet to allow others to access it.

If you want people to be able to view but not interact with your database, you can export all or part of a table as a static HTML *(Hypertext Markup Language)* page (**Figure 2.8**) that's viewable by anyone with a Web browser. If you prefer that the data be live and interactive, you can publish it as a *data access page* that's accessible via a Web browser.

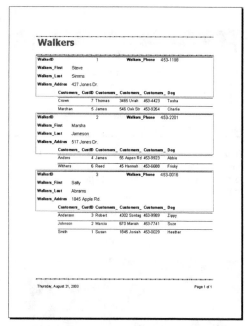

Figure 2.6 Reports present data in ways that make it simple to understand and draw conclusions.

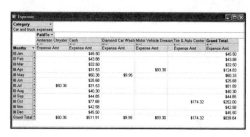

Figure 2.7 This PivotTable shows the breakdown of car expenses by month.

Figure 2.8 You can create a static HTML table from any data table.

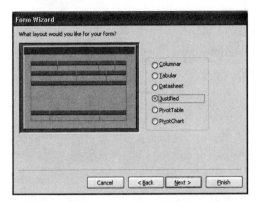

Figure 2.9 Wizards help you create new objects by presenting options to you in a series of dialog boxes.

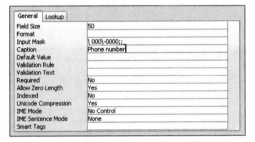

Figure 2.10 Open a table in Design View to examine or change field properties.

Wizards

Although you can manually design any table, form, chart, or report, Access provides tools called *wizards* that step you through the process. For example, if you'd rather not draw fields on a blank layout to create a custom form, the Form Wizard (**Figure 2.9**) allows you to select fields from lists and then automatically arranges them in one of several predefined layouts.

Until you become adept at manually designing Access objects, it's a good idea to take advantage of the wizards. Even if the wizard result isn't perfect, it's often easier to edit it than to create an object from scratch.

Objects, controls, and properties

Every major element in Access is an *object*—whether it be a table, form, report, query, data access page, or macro. The types of objects that you can create are listed in the Database window.

Controls are placed within objects. Examples include fields, list boxes, and option groups for collecting data. Controls such as these that have a specific data source are called *bound controls*. Static text, lines, and other elements that are not tied to a data source are called *unbound controls*.

Objects and controls all have *properties* that you can set or modify. Examples of properties include Format, Decimal Places, and Width (for a field on a form); and On Click and Display When (for a button on a switchboard). To view or alter the properties of any object and its controls, open the object in Design View.

✔ Tip

- To modify critical properties of a field (such as its length or data type), open its table in Design View (**Figure 2.10**). This is also where you create and delete fields.

The Access Interface

The following sections explain the parts of the Access interface and how to use them.

The Startup Task Pane

When you launch Access from the Start menu, the Startup Task Pane (**Figure 2.11**) is the first thing you see. (Note that if you launch Access by opening a database, the Startup Task Pane doesn't appear.) You can initiate the following tasks by clicking text links in the pane:

◆ View training materials from Office Online

◆ Search for help on a topic by entering a keyword, phrase, or question

◆ Open a recently used database by clicking its file name

◆ Open any other database by clicking More

◆ Create a new database

After opening a database, the Startup Task Pane automatically closes. You can also close the pane manually by clicking its close box.

✔ Tip

■ If you'd rather not see the Startup Task Pane when you launch Access, choose Tools > Options, click the View tab, and remove the checkmark from Startup Task Pane (**Figure 2.12**).

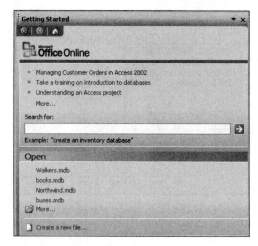

Figure 2.11 You can open a database, create a new database, or request help in the Startup Task Pane.

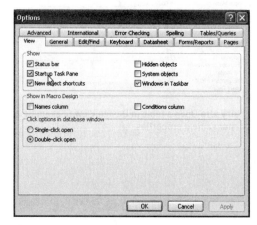

Figure 2.12 You can turn off the automatic display of the Startup Task Pane.

Object categories   *Objects and commands*

Figure 2.13 Select an object category from the list on the left and then double-click an object or command in the list on the right.

The Database window

After you open a database, the most important component of the Access interface appears: the Database window (**Figure 2.13**). Think of it as Access Command Central. From the Database window, you can open datasheets, forms, reports, and queries for data entry, viewing, or design changes.

Down the left side of the window is the Objects list. Click an object category to list all defined objects of that type in the right side of the window. To open a listed item, double-click it. Other things that you can do in the Database window include the following:

♦ Create a new object of the selected type (Forms or Reports, for example) by clicking the New toolbar icon or by double-clicking any of the Create entries in the right-hand side of the window.

♦ Delete any database object that's no longer needed. Select the object, and either click the Delete toolbar icon or press Del.

♦ Change the design of any object (adding fields to a table, changing field data types, or modifying a form, for example). Select an object and click the Design toolbar icon.

♦ Change the name of an object by right-clicking it and choosing Rename.

✔ Tips

■ Closing the Database window is the same as closing the current database. Leave it open or minimized until you're ready to close the current database.

■ Only one database can be open at a time. Normally, you will close the current database before opening another. If you need to view multiple databases, you can run multiple Access sessions by opening additional databases from the Desktop.

THE ACCESS INTERFACE

Menus and toolbars

Menus and toolbars in Access work as they do in other Windows applications. For instance, as you switch from one task to another, Access automatically displays appropriate menus and toolbars. There are, however, two differences.

The first difference is that—in order to prevent new users from being overwhelmed by the number of commands in each menu—Access can present abbreviated menus that show only the commands you've recently used (**Figure 2.14**). The behavior of the Expand indicator at the bottom of each menu is governed by a setting on the Options tab of the Customize dialog box (**Figure 2.15**).

The second difference is that Access actively tracks the commands and toolbar elements that you use. This data is used to continually modify the menus and toolbars to match your usage patterns.

✔ Tips

■ To change the toolbars that are displayed, choose Tools > Customize, click the Toolbars tab of the Customize dialog box, and check the toolbars that you want to show.

■ In Access, you can customize the standard toolbars and menus, as well as create new ones. For instructions, refer to Chapter 20.

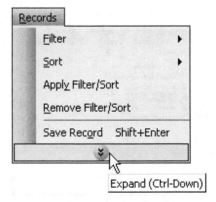

Figure 2.14 To expand an abbreviated menu, click this Expand indicator or rest the cursor on it (depending on the settings in the Customize dialog box shown in Figure 2.15).

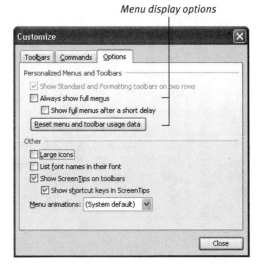

Figure 2.15 You can choose between showing full and abbreviated menus. With abbreviated menus, you can also set how they will expand: automatically or only when clicked.

THE ACCESS INTERFACE

Figure 2.16 This text box is always available for help questions.

Figure 2.17 This Office Assistant text box can also be used to request help.

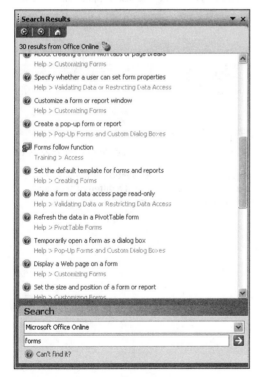

Figure 2.18 Results of all help searches appear as entries in this Search Results pane.

Requesting Help

Regardless of where you are in Access at the moment, there are several ways for you to request assistance. While you will usually enter search questions and phrases for Microsoft Office Access Help (described below), you can also do the following:

- ◆ In the top section of the Startup Task Pane (see Figure 2.11), click a tutorial topic.

- ◆ To visit Microsoft's Web site, choose Help > Microsoft Office Online.

After you've begun using the program, you'll find that most of the help information is in Microsoft Office Access Help. Access offers many ways for you to open and search for information in Microsoft Office Access Help, as described in the following lists.

To request assistance from Microsoft Office Access Help:

1. *Do one of the following:*

- ▲ Open the Access Help pane by choosing Help > Microsoft Office Access Help, pressing F1, or clicking the Microsoft Office Access Help toolbar icon. Then type a question or search string in the Search for text box.

- ▲ In the top section of the Startup Task Pane (see Figure 2.11), enter a search string in the text box.

- ▲ Type a question or search string in the box at the top of the document window (**Figure 2.16**).

- ▲ Click the Office Assistant, type a question or search string in its text box (**Figure 2.17**), and click Search. (If the Office Assistant isn't visible, choose Help > Show the Office Assistant.)

Results are displayed in the Search Results pane (**Figure 2.18**).

continues on next page

REQUESTING HELP

2. *Do any of the following:*

▲ To review a result, click the blue text link. The help text appears in a new pane (**Figure 2.19**).

▲ Click any gray text link that's preceded by *Help* > to open the Table of Contents to that help entry,

▲ To go forward or backward through the pane pages you've viewed, click the arrow icons at the top of the pane.

▲ To change the help source being searched (switching from Microsoft Office Online to Offline Help, for example), click the down-arrow in the Search section of the pane, choose the help material to search, and click the Start Searching button (**Figure 2.20**).

3. With the help text displayed (see Figure 2.19), you can do any of the following:

▲ Click any blue text string to view the word or phrase's definition.

▲ Click any blue topic that's preceded by a triangle to show/hide the topic text.

▲ Click Show All/Hide All to show or hide all topic text and definitions.

▲ Click the Print icon at the top of the pane to print the help text. (Expand any desired topics or definitions prior to clicking the Print icon.)

✔ Tip

■ To avoid paper waste, you can restrict help printouts to only selected text. Click and drag within a help topic to select text, click the Print icon, and then click the Selection radio button in the Print Range section of the Print dialog box.

Print the topic   *Expand all text*

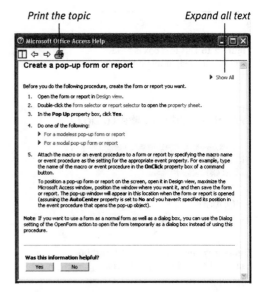

Figure 2.19 A clicked Help result appears in this pane.

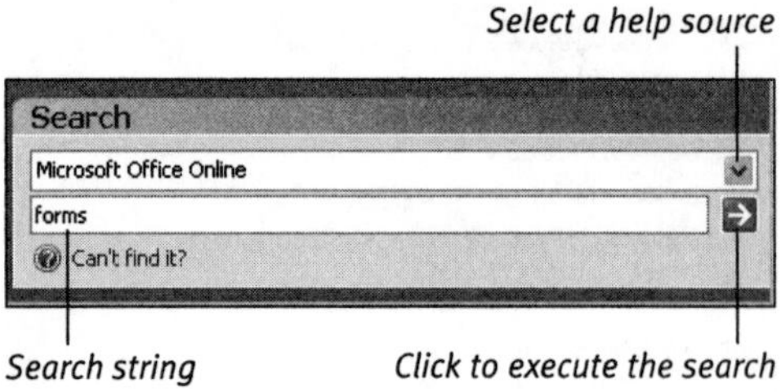

Select a help source

Figure 2.20 In the Search section of the Search Results pane, you can select a different source of help information to search.

Search string   *Click to execute the search*

REQUESTING HELP

CREATING DATABASES

In many instances, you'll find yourself working with an existing Access database that was designed and given to you by a friend, coworker, or supervisor. You probably won't be expected—or allowed—to customize the database. Instead, your time will be spent creating and deleting records, entering and editing data, sorting, searching, and generating reports.

However, it's also likely that you'll eventually want to create databases of your own. There will come a time when other people's databases won't meet your needs. While creating and customizing a database is more difficult than simply using someone else's, Access provides several methods of expediting the process. In this chapter, you'll learn to use the following techniques to create a new database:

- From a template, guided by a wizard
- By duplicating an existing database
- By designing its tables (using a wizard, entering data into a blank table, or from scratch in Design View)

Regardless of the method you choose, creating a database requires—at a minimum—that you name the database file, create at least one table, and specify a preliminary set of fields for the table.

Opening the New File Pane

All new databases are created by choosing a command from the New File pane. You can use any of the following techniques to open the pane.

To open the New File pane:

◆ *Do one of the following:*
   ▲ Click the New toolbar icon (**Figure 3.1**).
   ▲ Choose File > New.
   ▲ Press Ctrl N.
   The New File Pane appears (**Figure 3.2**).

✔ Tips

■ Depending on what you're currently doing in Access, the New toolbar icon may or may not be displayed. However, you can *always* choose File > New or press Ctrl N.

■ If you've just launched Access without simultaneously opening a database, there's another way to open the New File pane. In the Getting Started pane (**Figure 3.3**), click Create a new file.

New toolbar icon

Figure 3.1 You can open the New File pane by clicking the New toolbar icon.

Figure 3.2 All new databases are created by choosing a command from the New File pane.

Open the New File pane

Figure 3.3 You can also open the New File pane from the Getting Started pane.

OPENING THE NEW FILE PANE

Databases tab   Preview

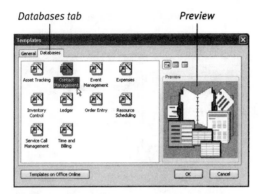

Figure 3.4 Select a database template and click OK.

Figure 3.5 Select a location for the database, name it (or accept the proposed name), and then click Create.

Table list   Required and optional fields

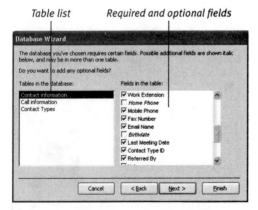

Figure 3.6 To review the required and optional fields that will be created, click each of the table names.

Creating a Database from a Template

If one of the provided Access templates matches the type of database you want, this construction option will do all the work for you. It will create the necessary tables and relationships, lay out the forms and reports, and even create a Switchboard you can use to perform common activities. A wizard helps you customize the database by specifying optional fields, as well as styles for the generated forms and reports.

To create a database from a template:

1. In the Templates section of the New File pane (see Figure 3.2), click On my computer.
   The Templates dialog box appears.

2. Select a template from the Databases tab (**Figure 3.4**).
   When you click the file icon for a template, a graphic preview of the database's forms and reports appears in the right side of the Templates dialog box.

3. To create a database from the selected template, click OK.
   The File New Database dialog box appears (**Figure 3.5**).

4. Navigate to the drive and folder in which you want to store the database, enter a name for it (or accept the default name that is proposed), and click Create.
   The Database Wizard appears.

5. Click Next.
   The list of tables to be created is shown in the left side of the wizard (**Figure 3.6**).

6. One by one, select each table name.
   The list of required fields (checked, normal type) and optional fields (unchecked, italic) is shown in the right side of the wizard.

continues on next page

7. Enter a checkmark for any optional field that you'd like to add to the currently selected table and click Next.

8. Select a style to be used to format forms (**Figure 3.7**) and click Next.

9. Select a style to be used to format reports (**Figure 3.8**) and click Next.

10. Enter a title for the database (**Figure 3.9**). The title will be used to label all Switchboard windows.

11. To insert a picture (such as a company logo) into your reports, click the check box, and then click the Picture button. Select a picture from your hard disk or any other connected drive, and then click OK.

    A thumbnail of the selected picture is displayed in the dialog box.

12. Click Next.

13. *Optional:* To immediately begin using the database, click the Yes, start the database check box.

14. Click Finish.

    Access constructs the database.

✔ Tip

■ Useful Access templates can sometimes be found online. In the Templates section of the New File pane (see Figure 3.2), click Templates home page. Your Web browser will launch and open to Microsoft Office Online. To use a downloaded template (from Microsoft or any other source) as the basis for a new database, follow the instructions presented in "Duplicating an Existing Database," in the next section.

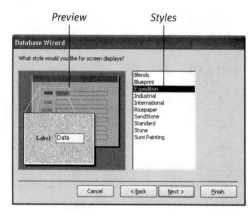

Figure 3.7 Select a form style/format from the list.

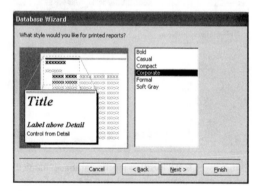

Figure 3.8 Select a report style/format.

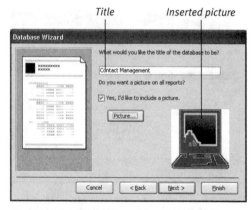

Figure 3.9 Enter a database title and, if you wish, select a picture to be used in all reports.

Figure 3.10 Select an existing database or template in this file dialog box.

Duplicating an Existing Database

You can use any Access database as the basis for another database. When you create a database from an existing file, Access generates an exact duplicate of the original—containing the same forms, reports, and records.

This procedure is extremely useful in two cases:

◆ When you need a backup copy of a database for security purposes

◆ When you need a fresh copy of a database that you regularly begin anew (such as a call record database that you purge or archive daily, weekly, monthly, or annually)

To create a new database from an existing database:

1. In the New section of the New File pane (see Figure 3.2), click From existing file.

   The New from Existing File dialog box appears (**Figure 3.10**).

2. Navigate to the folder in which the existing database or template is stored, and then click its filename.

   A copy of the database or template is stored in the same folder, and the copy opens. A number is appended to the new filename to distinguish it from the original. For example, choosing *Contacts.mdb* would result in a database named *Contacts1.mdb*. If multiple copies already exist in the folder, the next higher number will be appended.

✔ Tips

■ In addition to creating usable copies of your own databases, you can also use this procedure to create working copies of templates that you've downloaded or been given.

■ If your intent is to create an empty copy of a database, you will need to delete any old records from the copy.

Creating a Database by Designing Tables

Every Access database must contain at least one table and its associated field definitions. When you create a new database from a template or by duplicating an existing database, the tables are automatically generated for you. However, if you want greater control over the design of a given database, you can create your own tables in any of these ways:

♦ Use a wizard to select fields from ones suggested (similar to creating a database from a template, but with more options).

♦ Enter actual data directly into a blank datasheet and have Access define the fields based on your entries.

♦ Manually specify the field definitions.

Note that the techniques discussed in this section can also be used to create *additional* tables for an existing database. Here, however, the assumption is that you are using them to create the *first* table for a new database, effectively creating the database at the same time.

Selected object type   Table creation options

Figure 3.11 You use the Database window to define and edit tables, forms, reports, and other database objects.

Table list   Possible fields   Selected fields

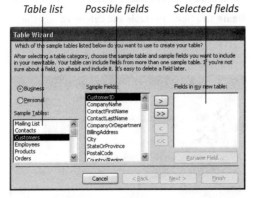

Figure 3.12 Use the Table Wizard to select a type of table to create and the fields to use.

Creating a table with the wizard

You'll find that using the Table Wizard is similar to creating a database based on a template. Rather than having to manually name fields and specify field definitions, you choose fields from a set that's appropriate for a particular type of database.

To create a database using the Table Wizard:

1. In the New section of the New File pane (see Figure 3.2), click Blank database.

   The File New Database dialog box appears (see Figure 3.5).

2. Navigate to the drive and folder in which you want to store the database, name it (or accept the proposed name), and click Create.

   The Database window appears (**Figure 3.11**).

3. Select Tables in the Objects section of the Database window and then double-click Create table by using wizard.

   The Table Wizard appears (**Figure 3.12**).

4. Click the Business or Personal radio button, depending on the type of table you want to create.

   The Sample Tables list displays a list of either business or personal database tables, as appropriate.

5. Select a table from the Sample Tables list.

   A list of potential fields appears in the Sample Fields list box.

6. From the Sample Fields list, select each field that you want to include in the table. Select fields in the order that you want them to appear in the datasheet.

   To move a single field into the Fields in my new table list, click the > button or double-click the field name. To simultaneously add *all* fields, click the >> button.

continues on next page

7. You can also add fields from other sample tables by repeating Steps 4–6, if you wish.

8. To remove one or several selected fields from the Fields in my new table list, click the < button. To completely clear the list, click the << button.

9. *Optional:* To rename a field in the Fields in my new table list, select it and click the Rename Field button.

The Rename field dialog box appears (**Figure 3.13**). Enter a new name for the field and click OK.

10. When you're satisfied with the selected fields, names, and their order, click Next.

11. In the new dialog box (**Figure 3.14**), name the table and click a radio button to indicate whether you or Access will create the *primary key* (the field whose contents will uniquely identify each record in this table).

12. Click Next to continue.

The final dialog box appears (**Figure 3.15**).

13. Click a radio button to indicate what you want to do next: manually edit the table design (by altering field definitions, for example), begin entering data into the table's datasheet, or ask Access to create a data entry form for the table.

14. Click the Finish button.

15. To create additional tables and specify the relationships among them, return to the Database window and repeat Steps 3–14. If you prefer, you can use one of the other table design methods discussed later in this section.

✔ Tips

■ It's best to use the Rename feature only for renaming fields. If you use it to *replace* a field—even if it's with a field of the same type—the database may not work properly.

Figure 3.13 Enter a new name for the field, and then click OK.

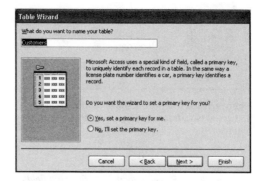

Figure 3.14 Name the table and determine how the primary key will be created.

Figure 3.15 Select an action to take after Access has finished creating the table.

■ If the database will contain only one table (that is, it is not relational), you may have no use for a primary key field. It isn't required.

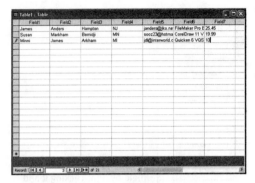

Figure 3.16 Another way to create a database is to just enter data into a blank datasheet.

Figure 3.17 Since this is a new table, you must name and save it.

Creating a table from a blank datasheet

Using this method, you simply start entering data into an empty datasheet. As you do, Access analyzes the data in each field and tries to assign appropriate data types and formats. While this isn't as accurate as allowing the Table Wizard to perform its magic, it's an excellent middle-of-the-road option, especially when none of the Table Wizard's sample tables are suitable for your project.

To create a table from a blank datasheet:

1. In the New section of the New File pane (see Figure 3.2), click Blank database.

   The File New Database dialog box appears (see Figure 3.5).

2. Navigate to the drive and folder in which you want to store the database, enter a name for it (or accept the default name that is proposed), and click Create.

   The Database window appears (see Figure 3.11).

3. Select Tables in the Objects section of the Database window and then double-click Create table by entering data.

   A blank datasheet appears.

4. Enter data for several records, making sure that you do so consistently (**Figure 3.16**).

5. Save the table by doing any of the following:
   ▲ Click the Save toolbar icon.
   ▲ Choose File > Save or press Ctrl S.
   ▲ Close the datasheet by clicking its *close box* (the X in the upper-right corner).

   A Save As dialog box appears (**Figure 3.17**).

6. Name the table and click OK.

   A dialog box appears, giving you an opportunity to create a primary key for the table.

   continues on next page

7. *Do one of the following:*

   ▲ Click Yes to instruct Access to create the primary key (an AutoNumber field).

   ▲ Click No if you don't want a primary key or if you wish to specify one manually. For example, you may already have defined a field (such as Part Number or Social Security Number) that you mean to use as the primary key.

   The datasheet closes and the Database window becomes active.

8. Open the new table by double-clicking its name in the Database window.

   You'll note that the fields still have their default names: Field1, Field2, and so on.

9. To rename a field, do either of the following:

   ▲ Right-click the field name and choose Rename Column from the pop-up menu that appears (**Figure 3.18**).

   ▲ Double-click the field name.

   The field name is selected (**Figure 3.19**). Type a new field name, overwriting and replacing the default one.

✔ Tip

■ While the assigned data types and formats represent Access' best guesses, it's not unusual for some of them to be incorrect. For instance, in the table shown in Figure 3.16, Access defined Field7 to be of type Number rather than Currency. (Number would still work, but Currency is more accurate.) As a result, you may want to open the new table in Design View, check the data type assigned to each field, and change them as needed.

Figure 3.18 You can rename a field by right-clicking it and choosing Rename Column.

Selected field name

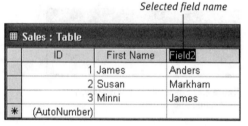

Figure 3.19 After the field name is selected, you can rename it by simply typing over the old name.

Field Name Data Type *Optional descriptive text*

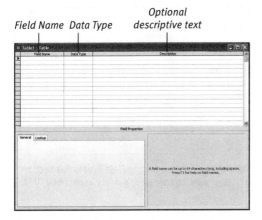

Figure 3.20 In Design View, you're on your own; there are no wizards to guide you. However, the lower-right corner of the window presents extremely helpful hints and explanations.

Click to choose a field type

Field Name	Data Type
Salary	Text
	Text
	Memo
	Number
	Date/Time
	Currency
	AutoNumber
	Yes/No
	OLE Object
	Hyperlink
	Lookup Wizard...

Figure 3.21 If Text isn't the correct type for the current field, you can choose another data type from this drop-down list.

Creating a table manually

While this table design method affords you the greatest control, it is also the most difficult—especially for novice Access users. Using this method, you will be working in Design View for the first time—defining each field that will be included in the new table. If you later need to make changes to this or any other table, they'll also be done in Design View.

To manually create a table:

1. In the New section of the New File pane (see Figure 3.2), click Blank database.

    The File New Database dialog box appears (see Figure 3.5).

2. Navigate to the drive and folder in which you want to store the database, enter a name for it (or accept the default name that is proposed), and click Create.

    The Database window appears.

3. Be sure that Tables is selected in the left side of the Database window and then double-click Create table in Design View.

    A blank table appears, opened in Design View (**Figure 3.20**). The insertion mark is positioned in the first blank Field Name cell.

4. Type the name of the first field that you want to create.

    As indicated in the lower-right area of the window, a field name may contain up to 64 characters—including spaces.

5. Press [Tab] when you're done entering the field name.

    The insertion mark moves to the Data Type column for the current field. By default, Text is proposed as the data type.

6. To select a different data type for the field, click the down arrow (**Figure 3.21**), and then choose the desired data type from the drop-down list.

continues on next page

CREATING A DATABASE BY DESIGNING TABLES

7. *Optional:* Press [Tab] to move to the Description column, and enter text to describe the field.

A field's Description automatically appears in the status bar when you're entering or editing data in that field.

8. *Optional:* To set additional options for the field, such as fixing the number of decimal places or creating a different field label (Caption), make the necessary changes in the Field Properties section at the bottom of the window (**Figure 3.22**).

9. To define additional fields, press [Tab] to move to the next blank Field Name box. Repeat Steps 4 through 8.

10. To save the new table, click the Save toolbar icon, choose File > Save, or press [Ctrl][S].

A Save As dialog box appears (see Figure 3.17).

11. Name the table and click OK.

A dialog box appears, giving you an opportunity to create a primary key for the table.

12. *Do one of the following:*

▲ Click Yes to instruct Access to create the primary key (an AutoNumber field).

▲ Click No if you don't want a primary key or if you wish to specify one manually. For example, you may already have defined a field (such as Part Number or Social Security Number) that you mean to use as the primary key.

The new table is saved.

✔ Tip

■ Defining and modifying fields is discussed in much greater detail in Chapter 4. Primary key fields are explained in Chapter 7.

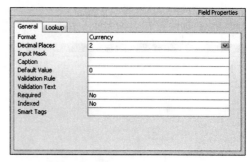

Figure 3.22 You can use the Field Properties section of the window to change or set any aspect of a field.

What Next?

What comes next for your new database depends largely on the creation method you used and how thorough it was.

Only the wizard-guided template method (see "Creating a Database from a Template," earlier in this chapter) will produce a database that is 100 percent ready to use. All tables, fields, and relationships have been defined; and all forms and layouts have been created for you. A template-generated database is immediately ready to receive data.

Only a shade behind the template method is that of basing the new database on an existing database or template (see "Duplicating an Existing Database," earlier in this chapter). If the original database or template was satisfactory, all you'll have to do to prepare the copy for data entry is delete any records it contains.

Databases generated by choosing the Blank Database command (see "Creating a Database by Designing Tables," earlier in this chapter) will require the most work. Since each of the methods associated with this command only creates the first table for you, any of these additional steps may be necessary:

◆ Modifying field definitions, deleting unnecessary fields, and adding others

◆ Creating additional tables and specifying the relationships between them

◆ Modifying the datasheets (by changing the font, altering column widths, or rearranging columns, for example)

◆ Designing forms and reports

Unless your needs are minimal, you'll find that it is time consuming to create a solid, working database that provides needed information in a useful form. Don't be surprised if the material covered in this chapter is frequently only the first step in a lengthy refinement process.

✔ Tips

■ Regardless of whether you feel that your new database needs some adjustments, you can still begin entering data, if you wish. Entering a few sample records is an excellent way to quickly uncover needed changes to the structure of a new database.

■ Although they're usually a desirable addition, no database requires custom forms. If you don't mind its lackluster format, you can enter data directly into any table's datasheet.

WHAT NEXT?

TABLES AND FIELDS

In Chapter 3, you learned the various ways that you can create databases and, as part of the process, create tables. This chapter also discusses tables, but focuses on the components of tables; that is, *fields*.

In this chapter, you'll learn to do the following:

- ◆ Set and change the data type for a field
- ◆ Create lookup fields
- ◆ Set common field properties
- ◆ Create an input mask to ensure consistent data entry and display formatting
- ◆ Create field validation rules
- ◆ Add and delete fields

About Data Types

The basic element of every table is the field. Each field is meant to record a particular kind of data (known as its *data type*). By assigning a data type to a field, you're setting rudimentary validation criteria for the field. For example, entering text in a Currency field triggers an error message (**Figure 4.1**).

Data types are assigned when you create a new database, add a new table, or add fields to an existing table. The data type for any field can be changed, if necessary, but this can sometimes result in data loss or unusual results. If there's a potential problem converting to a new data type, Access will warn you.

Each field can be one of the following data types: Text, Memo, Number, Date/Time, Currency, AutoNumber, Yes/No, OLE Object, Hyperlink, or Lookup Wizard. The types and their requirements and limitations are explained in the following sections.

Text

In most databases, the majority of fields are Text. A Text field can store any combination of typed characters: letters, numbers, and punctuation. Many fields that are commonly thought of as numeric are, in fact, best created as Text fields. A zip code field is one such example. Because zip codes can have a leading zero (e.g., 01776), only by declaring them to be Text fields can the leading zero be preserved. Any Text field can contain up to 255 characters. Examples of Text fields include addresses, names, and purchase descriptions.

Memo

A Memo field is an extra large Text field (up to 65,535 characters), making it ideal for recording long comments and notes (**Figure 4.2**). When sorting on a Memo field, Access considers only the first 255 characters.

Figure 4.1 Choosing the proper data type for a field helps prevent incorrect data from being entered.

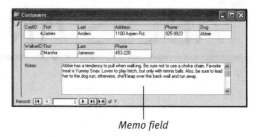

Memo field

Figure 4.2 This is an example of a Memo field.

Custom Field Formats

In addition to picking a display format from the predefined ones in the Format drop-down list, you can create a *custom format* for fields of any of the following data types: Text, Memo, Number, Currency, Yes/No, and Date/Time. For example, to force all text to lowercase in an Email Address field, all you have to do is enter < in the field's Format properties text box.

For help with creating custom formats, open a table in Design View, select any field, click in the Format properties box, and press F1.

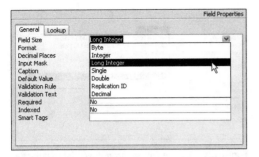

Figure 4.3 Open a table in Design View, select a Number field, and then open the Field Size drop-down list to specify a number type.

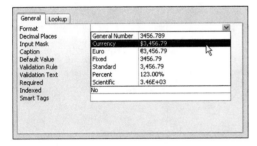

Figure 4.4 Click the Format drop-down list to select a display format for a Number or Currency field.

Indexing a Field

By default, new fields (other than an Auto-Number primary key) are not indexed. If you intend to regularly search or sort on a given field (especially in a *large* database), you can get a considerable speed increase by enabling indexing for the field. Which Yes option to pick depends on whether the values in the field must be unique. Select Yes (Duplicates OK) or Yes (No Duplicates).

Number

Use the Number data type to store most types of numeric data (with the exception of monetary amounts), especially numbers that you want to use in calculations. By setting the Field Size property (**Figure 4.3**) for a Number field, you can specify the type of numbers that will be stored—distinguishing between integer and decimal numbers, for example.

Currency

Currency is the other available data type for numeric data. It is the data type of choice for fields that record monetary amounts and is designed to prevent rounding errors. As with the Number data type, you can select a display format for data in a Currency field. Click the Format drop-down list when in Display View (**Figure 4.4**). To specify the number of decimal places to display, select an option from the Decimal Places drop-down list. (Note that this has no effect on the number of places that are *stored* for the number.)

AutoNumber

The AutoNumber data type is mainly used to automatically assign a new number to a primary key field, increasing the previously assigned number by one. Because an AutoNumber field must be unique within its table and kept in order, its Indexed field property is set to Yes (No Duplicates). Data in an AutoNumber field cannot be edited.

Although the default method of generating an AutoNumber is to increase the previous number by one for each new record you create, you can optionally instruct it to generate a random—yet still unique—number by setting its New Values property to Random.

Date/Time

Of course, a Date/Time field is used to store dates or times. Select a display format for a Date/Time field from the Format drop-down list (**Figure 4.5**).

Yes/No

Yes/No is the Access data type for recording *Boolean* data (in which only two opposing values are allowed). Yes/No fields can be formatted as Yes/No, True/False, or On/Off (although all are equivalent). By default, every Yes/No field is formatted as a single check box; checked is Yes, True, or On, unchecked is No, False, or Off.

OLE Object

Declaring a field as an OLE Object data type enables you to embed or link to documents created in other programs, such as Excel worksheets, images, or word processing files.

Embedded objects are static and are stored in the Access data file. *Linked objects* maintain a link to the original document and reflect any changes made to that document. Only a pointer or a reference to the original document is stored in the database.

Hyperlink

Declare a field as the Hyperlink data type so you can enter clickable addresses in the field. See **Table 4.1** for examples of some common address types that you can enter in a Hyperlink field.

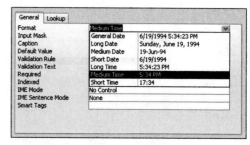

Figure 4.5 Click the Format drop-down list to select a display format for a Date/Time field. Note that such a field can hold either a date, a time, or both.

ABOUT DATA TYPES

Table 4.1

Examples of Hyperlink Formats

PURPOSE	PREFIX	EXAMPLES
Open browser to a Web page	http://	http://www.siliconwasteland.com or http://www.microsoft.com
Address a new email message	mailto:	mailto:roadrunner@bigriver.net
Open an FTP site to transfer files	ftp://	ftp://ftp.bigriver.net

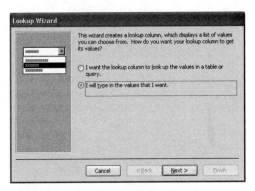

Figure 4.6 In the first dialog box, indicate whether the lookup will be based on values in an existing table/query or if you want to type the value list.

Hyperlink ─── Text that will appear in the field

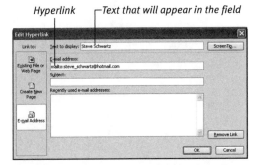

Figure 4.7 Use the Edit Hyperlink dialog box to create a new hyperlink to a Web page, email address, or file on disk. The appropriate prefix will automatically be entered for you.

Lookup Wizard

Defining a field as the Lookup Wizard type causes the field to display a drop-down list of values from which the user can choose. The values can be from another table, a query, or even from the same table. When you select Lookup Wizard as the data type, a series of dialog boxes appear to help you create the lookup (**Figure 4.6**).

✔ Tips

- If you're having trouble deciding between a Text field and a numeric field (Number or Currency), the deciding factor may be what you intend to do with the contents of the field. If you want to perform a computation based on the field's contents, choose a numeric data type.

- Text fields sort alphabetically, while numeric fields sort numerically. For instance, four street addresses in a Text field that begin with the numbers 4, 71, 115, and 1000 would sort as 1000, 115, 4, and 71.

- If you want to store lengthy documents in a field (especially formatted ones), use an OLE Object field rather than a Memo field.

- For help entering a correctly formatted hyperlink into a field, right-click the field and choose Hyperlink > Edit Hyperlink (**Figure 4.7**).

What About Calculations?

Amidst this discussion of data types, you may well be wondering about calculated fields and your ability to perform calculations within a datasheet. The answer is— you can't. There is no such field type or capability in a datasheet. Calculations are performed within queries.

ABOUT DATA TYPES

Setting Field Properties

For the most part, the default field properties will probably suffice. However, understanding what some of the key properties govern and how to set them can sometimes be very useful, providing the additional control you seek. Following are explanations of some of the properties that you may want to set or change.

Text field properties

◆ **Field Size.** The default field size for a Text field is a maximum of 50 characters. You can replace this with a smaller number, if you know that fewer characters will be needed. For instance, a Field Size of 2 would suffice for a State field (assuming that only two-character abbreviations are used).

◆ **Caption.** The caption serves as the field label. If no caption is entered, the field name is used.

◆ **Default Value.** If a particular text string will often be entered, you can make it the default (causing Access to automatically enter it for each new record). Of course, you can still replace it with other data after Access enters it. As an example, you might want to enter a default value for the City field in an Employee table.

The Default Value text must be enclosed in quotes. However, if you don't type the quotes, Access will enter them for you.

◆ **Indexed.** If you'll frequently sort on this field or include it in search criteria, indexing it will speed things up. Select "Yes (No Duplicates)" if values across all records must be unique; otherwise, choose "Yes (Duplicates OK)."

Memo field and Hyperlink field properties

◆ **Caption, Default Value, Indexed.** See "Text field properties."

Help with Field Properties

As you're setting properties for a selected field, minor explanatory text appears in the gray box in the bottom-right area of the window. For more specific help with most properties, you can press F1 to view the appropriate page in Microsoft Office Access Help.

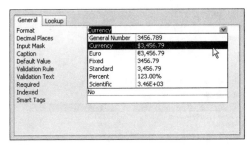

Figure 4.8 Select an appropriate currency format for the typical amounts you'll be entering.

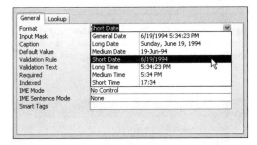

Figure 4.9 There are a several common date and time formats from which to choose.

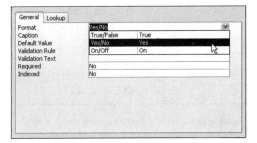

Figure 4.10 Select a Boolean format, depending on the kind of data that will be collected in the field.

Number field properties

◆ **Field Size.** This property governs the type of number that can be entered in the field.

◆ **Decimal Places.** This property controls how many decimal places are displayed (not stored) for the field. You can select a number to make Access display data in a consistent format, rounded off to that number of decimal places.

◆ **Caption, Default Value.** See "Text field properties."

Currency field properties

◆ **Format.** Currency is the most common format to choose. You may, however, prefer to pick a different display format, such as Standard (**Figure 4.8**).

◆ **Decimal Places.** See "Number field properties."

◆ **Caption, Default Value.** See "Text field properties."

Date/Time field properties

◆ **Format.** Select a date, time, or date/time display format from the drop-down list (**Figure 4.9**).

◆ **Caption, Default Value, Indexed.** See "Text field properties."

Yes/No field properties

◆ **Format.** Select a display format from the drop-down list (**Figure 4.10**).

◆ **Caption, Default Value.** See "Text field properties."

OLE Object field properties

◆ **Caption.** See "Text field properties."

SETTING FIELD PROPERTIES

Input Masks

The purpose of an *input mask* is to promote consistent data entry and result formatting. Rather than have phone numbers appear in a table field as (824) 453-1100, 824-453-1100, 824/453-1100, and 8244531100, you can use an input mask to ensure that only *one* of these formats is used for all entries. Text, Number, Date/Time, and Currency data types can have input masks. Access provides several common input masks from which you can choose, or you can create a custom mask.

To select or create an input mask:

1. Open a table in Design View.

2. Select a field by clicking its selector or by positioning the cursor in one of its columns.

3. Click in the Input Mask property at the bottom of the window, and then click the Build button (the ellipsis).

   The Input Mask Wizard appears (**Figure 4.11**).

4. Select a mask from the list.

5. Click in the Try It text box, position the insertion mark at the beginning of the list, and enter a data string. Click Next.

   The selected input mask is displayed (**Figure 4.12**).

6. *Optional:* Edit the input mask. You can also select a different *placeholder* (the character that is displayed during data entry to indicate where the user should type). If you edit the input mask, use the Try It text box to see if it works correctly. Click Next.

   The next wizard screen appears.

7. Click a radio button to select a data storage method. Click Next, and then click Finish in the final screen.

   Selecting "Without including the symbols…" can reduce disk storage requirements. And the field will still *display* the symbols.

Figure 4.11 In the first Input Mask Wizard screen, select a mask. (You can modify it in the next screen.) The Try It text box shows how it will appear to a user.

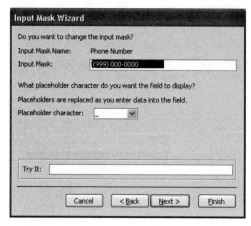

Figure 4.12 Modify the selected input mask, if you wish. You can also select a different placeholder character.

✔ Tips

- Input masks can also be created for fields in a query or on a form, as follows:

  ▲ To create an input mask in a query, switch to Design View, position the insertion mark in the field's column, click the Properties toolbar icon, and click the Build button to the right of the Input Mask item on the General tab.

  ▲ To create an input mask in a form, switch to Design View, select a field's text or combo box, click the Properties toolbar icon, and click the Build button to the right of the Input Mask item.

- When you create an input mask in Design View for a table, the mask is automatically applied to the same field when it's used in a query or form.

- To create a custom input mask, refer to "Input mask syntax and examples" in Microsoft Office Access Help. It provides a list of and explanations for all of the allowable mask characters. For example, a 0 is used to represent a required digit, while a 9 is used for an optional digit. Thus, you might design a phone number mask as (999) 000-0000.

- You can edit an input mask in the Input Mask box (found in the Field Properties section of the Design View window).

- Input masks govern the way you enter data and the manner in which it is displayed—*unless* you've also selected a Format property for the field. In that case, the Format setting takes precedence when displaying the data, but only after the record is saved.

Field Validation

Some items listed as Field Properties are meant to ensure that only appropriate data is entered in the field. Like setting a data type for each field, these items *validate* the data.

To set validation properties for a field:

1. Open a table in Design View.

2. Select a field by clicking its selector or by positioning the cursor in one of its columns.

3. *Optional:* Set the Required property to Yes to specify that the field is critical and cannot be left blank.

4. To create a validation rule, type an expression in the Validation Rule text box, or click the Build button to create a rule using the Expression Builder (**Figure 4.13**).

5. If you created a validation rule in Step 4, you can enter a Validation Text message that will be presented if the rule is violated (**Figure 4.14**).

    If you don't specify a message, a generic error dialog box will appear (**Figure 4.15**).

6. Close the window or switch to Datasheet View.

    Access will ask if you want to apply any new rules to existing data in the field(s).

7. Choose Yes to apply the rule to existing data (you'll be warned if any violations are found). Choose No to accept the rule(s), but only apply them to new data.

✔ Tips

- You can test new rules while still in Design View by right-clicking the table title and choosing Test Validation Rules.

- You can use And and Or to create complex rules, such as *>=0 And <=1000*.

- For help creating rules, search for *validation rules* in Microsoft Office Access Help.

Validation rule

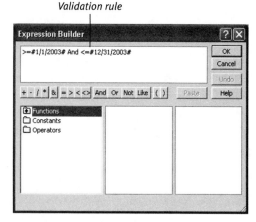

Figure 4.13 You can create a validation rule by typing and selecting options in the Expression Builder dialog box.

Figure 4.14 When a rule is validated, custom Validation Text can be shown.

Figure 4.15 If Validation Text hasn't been specified, Access merely displays the validation rule's expression. While it may not be clear to novices, it can suffice for more knowledgeable Access users.

FIELD VALIDATION

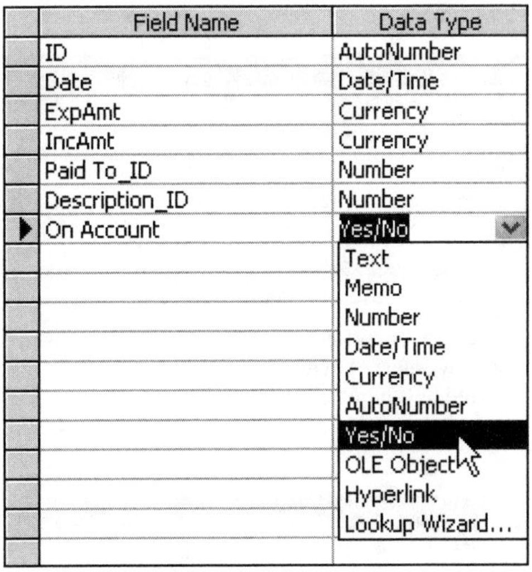

Field Name	Data Type
ID	AutoNumber
Date	Date/Time
ExpAmt	Currency
IncAmt	Currency
Paid To_ID	Number
Description_ID	Number
▶ On Account	Yes/No ▾
	Text
	Memo
	Number
	Date/Time
	Currency
	AutoNumber
	Yes/No
	OLE Object
	Hyperlink
	Lookup Wizard...

Figure 4.16 Part of the process of creating a new field in Design View is to set its data type.

Adding and Deleting Fields

In my experience, few databases are initially so well thought out that they don't go through many iterations. It's common to decide that additional fields are needed, as well as to chuck a few that weren't really necessary.

Creating new fields can be accomplished in Design or Datasheet View. Use the Datasheet View method when you're in a rush and a quick-and-dirty addition is all you need—at least for the moment. Use Design View when you also want to specify a data type and other field properties.

To add a new field in Design View:

1. Open a table in Design View.

2. *Do one of the following:*
   - ▲ Click in the first empty Field Name cell at the bottom of the table.
   - ▲ Click in the Field Name cell immediately below where you want to insert the field. Then choose Insert > Rows or click the Insert Rows toolbar icon.

3. Enter a name for the field.

4. Select a field type from the Data Type drop-down list (**Figure 4.16**).

5. *Optional:* Enter a description or comment in the Description cell.

6. *Optional:* Set or modify the field's properties in the text boxes at the bottom of the window, as explained previously in "Setting Field Properties."

7. If desired, add other new fields by repeating Steps 2–6.

8. When you're done adding fields, close the window. When prompted, save the changes.

To add a new field in Datasheet View:

1. Open a table in Datasheet View.

2. Select a column or a cell in a column. (The new column will appear to the left of the selected column/field.)

3. Choose Insert > Column.

   The new field appears (**Figure 4.17**).

4. *Optional:* You can rename the field by right-clicking its column label and choosing Rename Column.

   As an alternative, you can rename it at a more convenient time—when setting other field properties in Design View, for example.

To delete a field:

1. *Do any of the following:*

   ▲ In Datasheet View, click the column heading or a cell in the column, and then choose Edit > Delete Column.

   ▲ In Datasheet View, right-click the column and choose Delete Column (**Figure 4.18**).

   ▲ In Design View, select the field and choose Edit > Delete, choose Edit > Delete Rows, or press Del.

   ▲ In Design View, right-click anywhere within the field definition and choose Delete Rows.

   Regardless of the deletion method used, a confirmation dialog box appears.

2. Click Yes to complete the deletion.

✔ Tips

■ Sometimes the best way to add a field is to combine the two methods. Create the new field in Datasheet View and enter data in it for several records. Then switch to Design View and make any desired changes to the new field's properties.

New field

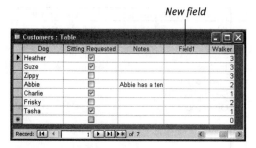

Figure 4.17 A new field is created to the left of the originally selected field. The default name is Field, followed by a number.

Figure 4.18 One way to delete a field from a table is to right-click it in Datasheet View and choose Delete Column.

■ In addition to creating the more typical field types, you can also add a Lookup or Hyperlink field. Instead of choosing Insert > Column, choose Insert > Lookup Column or Insert > Hyperlink Column.

Whenever you create a new table for a database, Access also generates a datasheet that you can use to view, enter, delete, and modify records. As you've seen in previous chapters, a *datasheet* is a spreadsheet-like display of data in which each row is a record and each column is a field (**Figure 5.1**). By default, the columns in a table's datasheet are presented in the order in which the fields were defined. If the table from which the datasheet is derived is related to other tables, it can display the related data as *subdatasheets* (**Figure 5.2**).

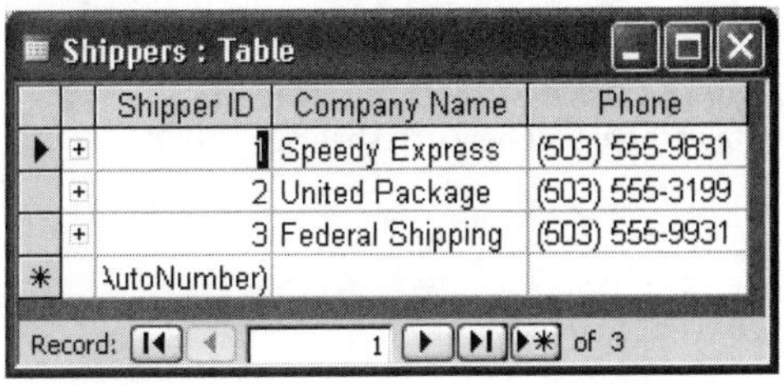

Figure 5.1 In Datasheet View, data is displayed in a spreadsheet-style grid. In this example, there are three fields (columns) and three records (rows).

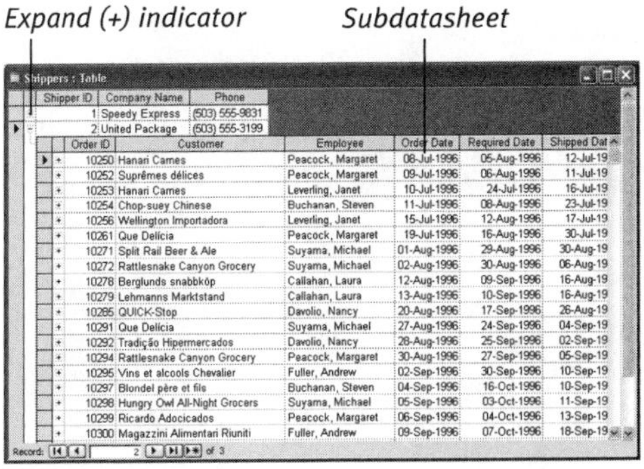

While datasheets are most commonly associated with tables, they can also appear in other places in an Access database. For instance, query results are displayed in a datasheet. You can also present any form as a datasheet. (To display a form as a datasheet, choose View > Datasheet View or choose Datasheet View from the View toolbar icon's drop-down menu, as shown in **Figure 5.3**).

Figure 5.2 Subdatasheet data for a given record can be exposed by clicking the record's expand (+) indicator.

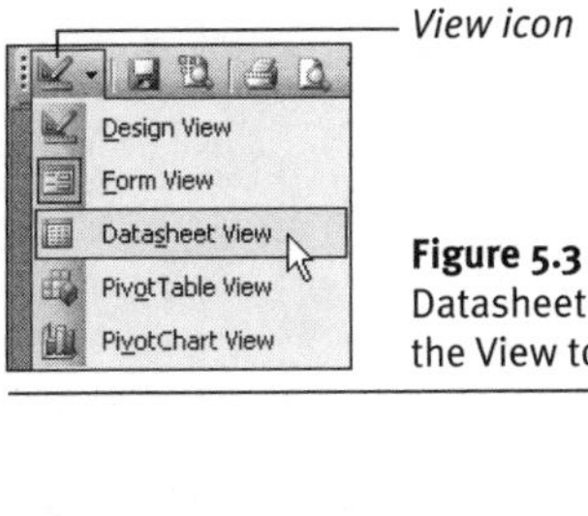

While the default formatting for a datasheet will often suffice, Access provides many ways for you to customize a datasheet. In this chapter, you'll learn to do the following:

◆ Set a default format for new datasheets

◆ Alter the formatting of existing datasheets

◆ Change row heights and column widths

◆ Hide, freeze, and move columns

Figure 5.3 You can switch to Datasheet View by clicking the View toolbar icon.

Setting a Default Format

Whenever you create a new datasheet, its cells and the data you enter are automatically displayed using the default colors, gridline settings, cell effect, and font. If you don't care for the drab look of Arial on a plain, unadorned grid (Access' default), you can specify your own default settings.

When you create new default settings, they affect every *new* datasheet generated for the database. Existing datasheets are unaffected.

To set a default format for new datasheets:

1. Choose Tools > Options.

   The Options dialog box appears (**Figure 5.4**).

2. Click the Datasheet tab.

3. Modify the settings as desired, and then click OK.

   New datasheets for the current database will conform to the settings. See the remaining sections of this chapter for discussions of the individual formatting options.

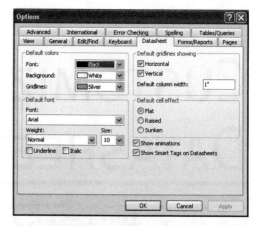

Figure 5.4 Use the Options dialog box to specify a default format for new datasheets.

Figure 5.5 Change settings in this dialog box to set the default formatting for all new datasheets.

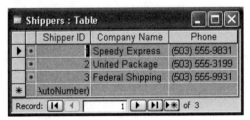

Figure 5.6 This is an example of the raised cell effect.

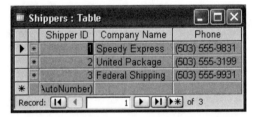

Figure 5.7 This is an example of the sunken cell effect.

Gridline and Cell Effect Formatting

You can customize the appearance of cells and gridlines in the current datasheet.

To set gridline and cell effects:

1. Open the datasheet that you want to format, and choose Format > Datasheet.

   The Datasheet Formatting dialog box appears (**Figure 5.5**). As you set formatting options, their effects are shown in the Sample box.

2. To specify a Raised (**Figure 5.6**) or Sunken (**Figure 5.7**) effect for the grid, click the radio button in the Cell Effect section.

   If you select any Cell Effect other than Flat (no effect), other formatting options cannot be set. Go to Step 6.

3. To hide the horizontal or vertical gridlines, click to remove their checkmarks in the Gridlines Shown section.

4. To set a new color for the cells or gridlines, choose them from the Background Color or Gridline Color drop-down list, respectively.

5. In the Border and Line Styles section, you can set different line styles for the datasheet border, horizontal and vertical gridlines, and the column header underline. For each one that you want to alter, select an item from the first drop-down list and then select a style from the second drop-down list.

6. Click OK.

✔ Tips

- To preserve applied formatting, you must save the datasheet. If you don't click the Save toolbar icon or choose File > Save, you'll be prompted to save when you close the datasheet.

- To restore the previous settings, reissue the Format > Datasheet command or close the datasheet without saving it.

Changing the Font

Each datasheet can have only a single font, size, style, and color. The font is used to format all text in the datasheet. Selective formatting— such as displaying a single word in a Comments field in italic—isn't supported.

To set a font, size, style, or color for a datasheet:

1. Open the datasheet that you want to format, and choose Format > Font.

   The Font dialog box appears (**Figure 5.8**). All installed fonts are listed.

2. Set options as desired.

   As you select options, their effects are shown in the Sample box.

3. Click OK.

   The new font settings are applied to the current datasheet.

✔ Tips

- Select a font, size, style, and color based on readability. Script and other "fancy" fonts are generally poor choices.

- Changes in font settings made for one data-sheet have no effect on others. If you want them all to match, you'll have to individually set them for each datasheet.

- As with other datasheet formatting options, you must save the datasheet to preserve the new fonts.

- There is no Undo available for reversing a font choice. You must reissue the Format > Font command. For this reason, before making a change, it's a good idea to note the original font, size, and style.

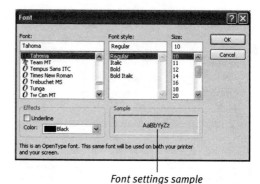

Font settings sample

Figure 5.8 Set new font options in the Font dialog box.

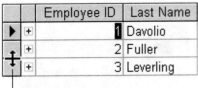

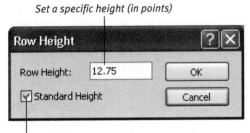

Row height cursor

Figure 5.9 You can set row height by dragging the bottom edge of any row.

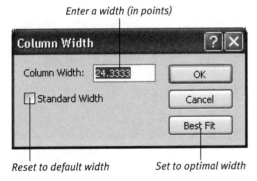

Set a specific height (in points)

Reset to default height

Figure 5.10 You can set the row height to the default or to a specific height (in points).

Enter a width (in points)

Reset to default width   *Set to optimal width*

Figure 5.11 There are several ways to set a column's width in this dialog box.

Setting Row Heights and Column Widths

You can also customize a datasheet by setting a new row height for all records or changing the widths of selected columns.

To set the row height for a datasheet:

1. Open the datasheet that you want to format.

2. *Do one of the following:*

   ▲ On the left side of the datasheet where the record selector is located, move the cursor over the line between any pair of records (**Figure 5.9**). Drag up or down to change the row height.

   ▲ Choose Format > Row Height. In the Row Height dialog box (**Figure 5.10**), enter a height (in points) or click the Standard Height check box.

   All rows in the datasheet will resize (other than the rows in embedded subdatasheets).

To change a column width:

1. Open the datasheet that you want to format.

2. *Do one of the following:*

   ▲ In the column headings area, move the cursor over the right edge of any field. Drag right or left to change the column's width.

   ▲ Double-click the right edge of a column heading to resize it to the optimal width. The column will expand or contract as needed in order to fully display the longest data string in the field.

   ▲ Position the cursor in any cell in the column, and choose Format > Column Width. In the dialog box (**Figure 5.11**), specify a width (in points), click the Standard Width check box to set the column to the default width, or click Best Fit in order to fully display the longest data string in the field. Click OK.

✔ Tips

- Changing the row height in a datasheet doesn't affect rows in subdatasheets. To set the row height for a subdatasheet, select a record in the subdatasheet (or in its own table/datasheet) and then adjust its height.

- Setting row height for a datasheet or subdatasheet also affects the table's display in other datasheets in which it appears.

- You can simultaneously set the widths of multiple adjacent columns. Select the columns (**Figure 5.12**), and then do one of the following:

  ▲ Double-click the right edge of one of the column headings to set them all to the optimal width.

  ▲ Choose Format > Column Width to set them all to the same width.

  ▲ Drag the right edge of one of the column headings to set them all to a new, uniform width.

Selected columns

Figure 5.12 To set the widths of multiple columns, start by drag-selecting their headings.

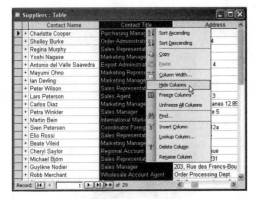

Figure 5.13 Right-click the heading of the column you want to hide and choose Hide Columns.

Hiding, Freezing, and Moving Columns

Another way that you can alter the appearance of a datasheet is by hiding unnecessary columns—making it easier to concentrate on the data that's important. You can also freeze selected columns so they remain onscreen as you scroll, as well as rearrange selected columns, if you wish.

To hide columns:

1. Open the datasheet that you want to format.

2. Select one or more contiguous columns by clicking their headings (see Figure 5.12).

3. *Do one of the following:*

   ▲ Choose Format > Hide Columns.

   ▲ If you're hiding a single column, right-click in the column and choose Hide Columns from the pop-up menu that appears (**Figure 5.13**).

   ▲ If you're hiding multiple columns, press [Shift] as you right-click the heading of the last selected column. Choose Hide Columns from the pop-up menu that appears.

   ▲ Hide the column manually by moving the cursor over the right edge of the column heading and then dragging to the left until the column disappears.

To freeze columns:

1. Open the datasheet that you want to format.

2. You can freeze one or more contiguous columns. Do one of the following:

   ▲ To select one column, click its heading.

   ▲ To select multiple columns, drag-select or (Shift)-click their headings.

3. *Do one of the following:*

   ▲ Choose Format > Freeze Columns.

   ▲ If you're freezing a single column, right-click its heading and choose Freeze Columns from the pop-up menu that appears (**Figure 5.14**).

   ▲ If you're freezing multiple columns, press (Shift) as you right-click the heading of the last selected column. Choose Freeze Columns from the pop-up menu that appears.

   The selected column(s) are moved to the left side of the datasheet. As you scroll the datasheet horizontally, the frozen columns remain visible.

To move a column to a new position:

1. Open the datasheet that you want to format.

2. *Do one of the following:*

   ▲ Click to select the column heading of the field that you want to move.

   ▲ To select multiple, contiguous columns, click the first column heading. Drag-select through the additional headings or (Shift)-click the final heading.

3. Drag the selected column heading(s) left or right to a new position (**Figure 5.15**). Release the mouse button to complete the move.

Selected column heading

Figure 5.14 Right-click the column heading that you want to freeze and choose Freeze Columns.

Destination   *Selected column*

Figure 5.15 You can drag one or more column headings to a new position. In this example, the Title of Courtesy column will precede the First Name column.

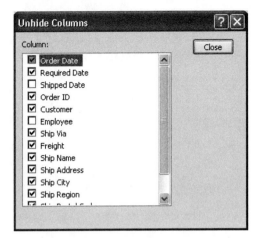

Figure 5.16 In the Unhide Columns dialog box, visible columns have checkmarks and hidden ones are unchecked.

✔ Tips

- To unhide one or more columns (making them visible again), choose Format > Unhide Columns. In the Unhide Columns dialog box (**Figure 5.16**), click the check boxes of the columns that you want to restore.

- You can also use the Unhide Columns dialog box to hide columns that are currently visible. Just remove their checkmarks.

- You can only freeze contiguous columns. If the columns that you want to freeze aren't next to each other, move them as necessary before issuing the Freeze Columns command.

- To unfreeze the columns, choose Format > Unfreeze All Columns or right-click anywhere in the datasheet and choose Unfreeze All Columns from the pop-up menu that appears.

- Unfreezing columns does not restore them to their original positions. You will have to manually move them back, if desired.

HIDING, FREEZING, AND MOVING COLUMNS

CREATING AND CUSTOMIZING FORMS

If you've experimented with datasheets, you've already discovered that they can sometimes be inconvenient to use for entering and viewing data. This is especially true when a table has many fields or many records.

To make data entry more pleasant, you can create *forms*—attractive layouts of fields, field labels, and static objects. You can create as many forms for your database as you need. Each can be based on selected fields from one or more tables and/or queries. The arrangement of fields and other items is entirely up to you. This chapter explains the various methods of creating and modifying data entry forms.

Note that switchboards, PivotCharts, and PivotTables are also Access form objects, even though their purpose isn't data entry. A *switchboard* is a custom, button-based user interface for an Access database. *PivotCharts* and *PivotTables* are data analysis tools, based on a statistic known as a crosstab. To learn about switchboards, see Chapter 19. PivotCharts and PivotTables are discussed in Chapter 13.

Creating Forms

As you learned in Chapter 3, some methods of creating a new database simultaneously generate forms, too. You can make additional forms by creating an AutoForm (based on all fields in one table or query), using the Form Wizard to create a customized form (based on selected fields from one or more tables or queries), or manually creating a form in Design View. Since working in Design View is the same whether you're creating or editing a form, it will be discussed in the next section.

To create an AutoForm:

1. Select Forms in the Objects area of the Database window.

2. Click the New toolbar icon or choose Insert > Form.

   The New Form dialog box appears (**Figure 6.1**).

3. Depending on the style wanted, select Auto-Form: Columnar or AutoForm: Tabular.

   You can also select AutoForm: Datasheet, but this merely creates a datasheet based on the selected form or query rather than creating a stylish form.

4. Select a table or query from which fields will be drawn.

   All fields from the selected table or query will be used to create the form.

5. Click OK to generate the form.

   The form is created and then opens (**Figure 6.2** and **Figure 6.3**).

6. Close the form after examining it.

   A dialog box appears, asking if you'd like to save the changes to the form design.

7. Click Yes, name the form in the Save As dialog box, and click OK.

   The form is added to the Database window as a new Forms object.

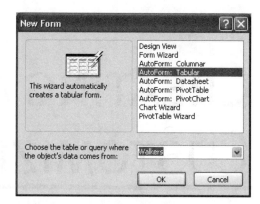

Figure 6.1 To create an AutoForm, you must open the New Form dialog box. Select an AutoForm style and a table or query on which to base the form.

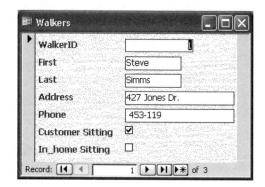

Figure 6.2 An example of an AutoForm: Columnar.

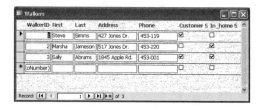

Figure 6.3 This is the same data table, created as an AutoForm: Tabular form.

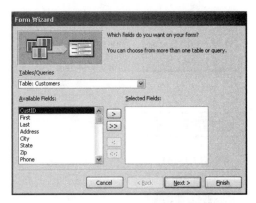

Figure 6.4 Select fields to include in the new form. The fields can be from multiple tables and queries.

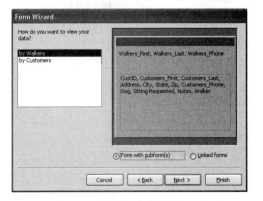

Figure 6.5 This grouping screen appears if you've chosen related fields from multiple tables.

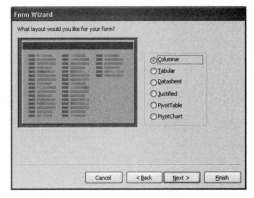

Figure 6.6 You can specify a field layout method for most forms.

To create a form with the Form Wizard:

1. Select Forms in the Objects area of the Database window.

2. Double-click Create form by using wizard. The Form Wizard appears (**Figure 6.4**).

3. From the Tables/Queries drop-down list, select the first table or query whose fields you want to use on the form.

   The Available Fields box displays all fields in the selected table or query.

4. Move the desired fields into the Selected Fields box. Click the > button to move a single selected field or the >> button to simultaneously move all fields.

   Note that the order of fields in the Selected Fields box determines the display order of fields in the completed form.

5. *Optional:* Repeat Steps 3 and 4 for other tables and queries from which you want to draw fields. Click Next to continue.

   As long as the tables are related, you can add fields from multiple tables/queries.

6. If you've chosen fields from multiple tables, a grouping screen appears (**Figure 6.5**). Select a view of the data from the list on the left, and select a form-creation method by clicking a radio button at the bottom (if any are presented). Click Next.

7. If you're creating anything other than linked forms, you'll be asked to select a layout method (**Figure 6.6**). The choices depend on the type of form(s) you're creating. Click a radio button, and click Next.

8. On the next screen, select a *form style* (background and field formatting). Click Next to continue.

9. On the final screen, name the form(s) and click Finish.

   The form is added as a new Forms object.

Editing Forms

Regardless of the method used to create a new form, you're free to change most of its elements. For example, you can move fields and labels to new positions, resize form sections, select different fonts and sizes for fields and labels, and change the form's background image. You can also add more elements, such as a picture or logo, graphic lines, and additional fields.

However, the procedures for making these modifications—even simple ones such as moving a label separately from its associated field—are often far from obvious. The remaining sections in this chapter will walk you through the process of making some common form modifications.

Selecting controls and other objects

To modify anything on a form (or the *entire* form), you must first select it.

To select an object on a form:

◆ *Do any of the following:*

▲ To select the entire form (to set form properties), click the small box at the intersection of the rulers (**Figure 6.7**). A black box indicates that it's selected.

▲ Click to select an individual item within a form, such as static text, a graphic, or a field and its label.

▲ To select multiple items, drag a selection rectangle around or through the items. You can also (Shift)-click each item.

▲ Click a form section's name (such as Detail or Form Footer) to select it.

▲ Select a specific object by selecting its name from the Object drop-down list on the toolbar (**Figure 6.8**). The currently selected object is also shown in this list.

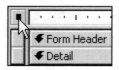

Figure 6.7 The black square indicates that the form is selected.

Figure 6.8 You can select any object on a form from the Object toolbar menu.

EDITING FORMS

Figure 6.9 Common formatting options, such as font, text alignment, and border style, can be selected from the Formatting (Form/Report) toolbar.

Move only the label

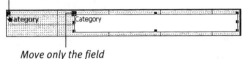

Move only the field

Figure 6.10 After selecting a field, you can move the field or label separately by dragging a black box.

Setting Properties

The form, form sections, and every object on the form have *properties* that you can modify. Many (such as font and color) can be set by choosing menu commands, clicking toolbar icons, or manually manipulating the object (to resize or reposition it, for example). Other properties can only be modified in the object's properties dialog box.

When in Design View, you can open the properties dialog box for a selected object by doing any of the following:

- ◆ Double-click the object or element
- ◆ Click the Properties toolbar icon
- ◆ Choose View > Properties
- ◆ Press (Alt)(Enter)

Options for selected objects

After selecting an object on a form, you can do any of the following:

- ◆ Move it to a new location on the form
- ◆ Change its size by dragging a handle
- ◆ Delete the object
- ◆ Change its formatting by selecting options from the Formatting (Form/Report) toolbar (**Figure 6.9**)
- ◆ Set or change other important object properties by clicking the Properties toolbar icon, choosing View > Properties, or by pressing (Alt)(Enter)

Moving objects

These are the important points about moving objects on a form.

- ◆ To move a field or another selected object, click and drag it to a new location. (When an object is ready to be moved, the cursor changes to an open hand.)
- ◆ To move a selected object a small distance, press an arrow key.
- ◆ A field and its label normally move together. To move *only* a field or a label, click the field and then move the cursor over the black square in the field or label's upper-left corner. The cursor changes to a pointing hand (**Figure 6.10**). After you move the field or label, the objects become a linked pair again.
- ◆ When Snap to Grid is enabled (Format > Snap to Grid), a moved object automatically snaps to the nearest grid intersection. (Placed objects also respect the grid.) To temporarily override grid snap, press (Ctrl) as you move the object.
- ◆ To constrain movements to only horizontal or vertical, hold (Shift) as you drag.

Resizing objects

You can change the size of selected objects on a form by dragging or choosing commands from menus. For example, a form generated using the Form Wizard or as an AutoForm can result in outlandish field sizes. You can resize the fields and labels, resulting in a more attractive and practical layout (**Figure 6.11**).

To resize an object:

1. Select the object by clicking it or by selecting its name from the Objects drop-down list on the Formatting toolbar.

2. *Do any of the following:*

    ▲ Drag one of the object's handles. When the cursor is a double arrow, you can drag (**Figure 6.12**).

    Drag the top- or bottom-center handle to change the height. Drag the left- or right-center handle to alter the width. Drag a corner handle to simultaneously change both the height and width.

    ▲ Open the properties dialog box for the object and change the Width and/or Height properties.

    ▲ If you select multiple objects, you can resize them all to match a common feature of one of the selected objects.

    Choose Format > Size > To Tallest, To Shortest, To Widest, or To Narrowest. If you choose To Narrowest, for example, the objects will all become the same width as the narrowest of the selected objects.

✔ Tip

■ If you select multiple objects and then drag a handle, all selected objects are resized by the same amount.

Original form

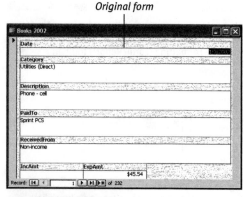

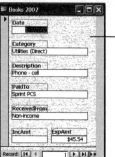

Form with resized fields and labels

Figure 6.11 Resizing fields and labels can greatly reduce the size of an Auto- or wizard-generated form.

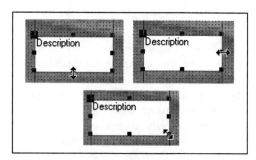

Figure 6.12 Drag a handle to change an object's height, width, or both dimensions.

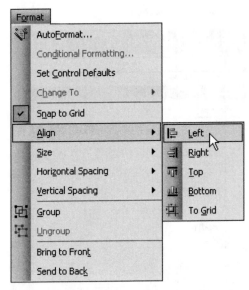

Figure 6.13 Choose an alignment command from the Format > Align submenu.

Aligning multiple objects

After moving or adding new elements to a form, you can align them to each other. Select the elements that you wish to align, and then choose a command from the Format > Align submenu (**Figure 6.13**).

Commands in the Format > Horizontal Spacing and Vertical Spacing submenus can be used to modify the spacing between selected elements. You can distribute the space evenly among the elements, reduce the space, or increase it. Select the elements that you wish to redistribute, and then choose a command from the appropriate submenu.

✔ Tips

■ With Snap to Grid enabled, you can also manually align elements.

■ The alignment commands can sometimes give unexpected results. To correct an unfortunate alignment choice, immediately choose Edit > Undo Align or press Ctrl Z.

Working with Form Sections

When you open a form in Design View, you'll note that it contains labeled horizontal bands. These bands mark the form's *sections* (**Figure 6.14**). From top to bottom, the following sections can be placed on a form:

◆ **Form Header.** The form header and the material it contains displays at the top of every record. If the forms are printed, it appears atop the first page. A form title or logo is often placed in the form header.

◆ **Page Header.** Material in the page header is only visible in printouts. The page header is printed at the top of every page.

◆ **Detail.** This section holds the data for each record. Fields are placed here.

◆ **Page Footer.** Like the page header, material in the page footer only appears in printouts (at the bottom of every page).

◆ **Form Footer.** The form footer and the material it contains displays at the bottom of every record.

Sections can be resized, added/removed, shown/hidden, and colored. To select a section for editing, click its bar or the selection box to the left of the bar.

To modify a selected section:

◆ *Do any of the following:*

  ▲ Change the height or width of a section by dragging its bottom or right edge, respectively (**Figure 6.15**). Change *any* section width to alter the form width.

  ▲ Add or remove the Form Header/Footer or the Page Header/Footer by choosing that command from the View menu.

  ▲ To hide a section, set its Visible property to No.

  ▲ To set a color for a selected section, click the Fill/Back Color toolbar icon.

Form Header section

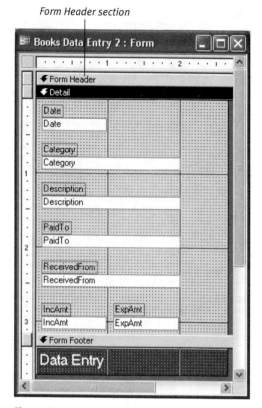

Figure 6.14 Each horizontal band marks the top of a form section.

Figure 6.15 When the cursor changes to a double arrow (at the bottom or right side of a section), you can drag to resize the section.

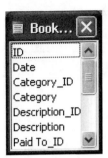

Figure 6.16 Select fields from the Field List.

Adding Objects to a Form

In addition to moving existing objects around on the form and changing their properties, you can add new items, such as additional fields, graphics, and static text.

✔ Tip

- To remove an object from a form, select it using any of the methods described in this chapter, and then choose Edit > Delete or press [Del].

Adding fields

To add fields to a form, you drag them from the Field List (**Figure 6.16**). If the Field List isn't visible, you can display it by choosing View > Field List.

You can drag individual fields onto a form or drag several as a group. To select multiple contiguous fields in the Field List, click the first one and then [Shift]-click the last one. To select noncontiguous fields, [Ctrl]-click each one.

✔ Tips

- When you release the mouse button after dragging a field into place, the left edge of the new field text box will correspond to the left edge of the dragged field icon. Leave room to the left of the field so that the label can be fully shown.

- You can only add fields that are present in the Field List. Every form is based on specific tables and queries from which the Field List is drawn. If you need to add other fields, you can either modify the tables/queries or create a new query that includes *all* the necessary fields.

- For help adding fields with more complex controls, such as lists, radio buttons, and check boxes, see "Adding special controls," later in this chapter.

ADDING OBJECTS TO A FORM

Adding other objects

You can embellish a form by adding static text (section and form titles, for example), graphics (images, lines, and boxes), or the current date and time.

To add other objects to a form:

◆ *Do any of the following:*

▲ **Date and/or time.** Choose Insert > Date and Time. Select options in the Date and Time dialog box (**Figure 6.17**), and click OK. A Date formula, Time formula, or both are inserted onto the form. The formulas continuously update the date and time.

▲ **Static text.** Select the Label icon in the Toolbox (**Figure 6.18**), click to set the insertion point on the form, type the text, and format it as desired.

▲ **Lines and rectangles.** Select the Line or the Rectangle icon in the Toolbox, click or click and drag to draw the object, and format it as desired.

▲ **Static image.** Choose Insert > Picture, select an image file from disk in the Insert Picture dialog box, and move the image where you want it to go. (You can also add a picture by selecting the Image icon in the Toolbox and then clicking a destination for it on the form.)

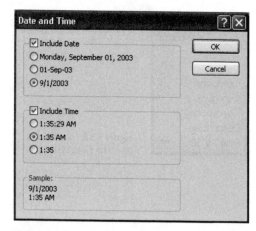

Figure 6.17 Enter a checkmark for each item that you want to include, and select a format for each one.

Figure 6.18 Most new items can be selected from the Toolbox.

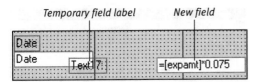

Temporary field label   New field

Figure 6.19 Enter an expression in the new field box.

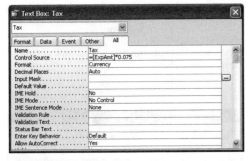

Figure 6.20 Set properties for the new field (such as its name and format) and for the field label.

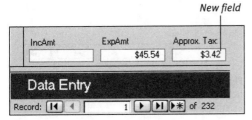

New field

Figure 6.21 Switch to Form View and examine the new field's contents in several records.

Using the Expression Builder

If you don't feel comfortable typing expressions by hand, you can use the Expression Builder. Click the Control Source property in the properties window, and then click the Build button to its right (the ellipsis). The Expression Builder lets you select fields and use any of Access' built-in functions to create complex expressions.

Adding calculations

As you saw in the discussion of Date/Time, forms can include calculations. You can create calculation expressions that combine field data, built-in functions, and constants to display record-specific data. Examples include a commission amount (computed by multiplying a sales total by a commission percentage) or the difference between an end and a start time (to display the amount of time spent on a phone call with a client).

To add a calculation to a form:

1. Select the Text Box icon in the Toolbox.

2. Click the spot on the form where you want the new field to appear.

   An unbound field is added to the form. Its name is Text *number*, such as Text12.

3. Click in the field, and type the expression (or use Expression Builder). For example, you could use *ExpAmt * 0.075* to calculate the state sales tax on a purchase, where ExpAmt is the sales total field and .075 is the tax percentage (7.5%).

   Access evaluates the expression and makes any necessary syntax corrections (**Figure 6.19**).

4. Select the field, and open its properties window (**Figure 6.20**).

5. Rename the field by replacing the temporary text in the Name property and, if appropriate, select a display format for the field from the Format list.

6. With the properties window still open, select the field label and change its Caption property to a more appropriate label. If you wish, you can also change the Name property.

7. Close the properties window and, if necessary, move the field and/or label to the desired position on the form (**Figure 6.21**).

Adding subforms

In addition to displaying individual fields from the source and related tables, you can add a subform to a form. A subform can display all matching related records from another table, for example (**Figure 6.22**).

To add a subform to a form:

1. Open the form in Design View.

2. Click the Subform/Subreport icon in the Toolbox, and click the form to set the subform's position.
   The Subform Wizard appears (**Figure 6.23**).

3. *Do one of the following:*
   ▲ To select specific fields to display in the subform, select Use existing Tables and Queries.
   ▲ To use all fields from another form, select Use an existing form.
   Click Next to continue.

4. If you selected Use existing Tables and Queries, you will be asked to specify the fields to use. You can select fields from a single table or query or from multiple tables and queries. Click Next to continue.

5. In the new screen (**Figure 6.24**), specify the matching field that links the form to the subform. Click Next to continue.

6. Enter a name for the subform. Click Finish. The subform and label appear on the form.

7. Make any necessary changes to the subform (resizing it, moving or deleting fields, and so on), and then switch to Form View to examine the results (see Figure 6.22).

✔ Tip

■ A subform can display one record at a time or a scrolling list of all matching records. Set its Default View property to Single Form or Continuous Forms.

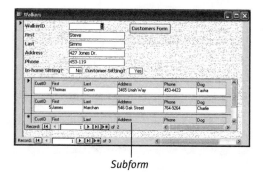

Subform

Figure 6.22 This subform lists all customers of the current dog walker.

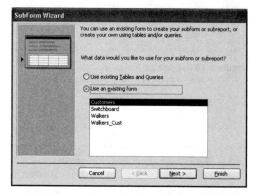

Figure 6.23 Indicate whether you want to select fields for the subform or use all of the ones from an existing table or query.

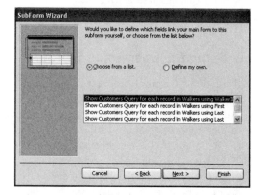

Figure 6.24 Specify the manner in which the main form and subform are linked to one another.

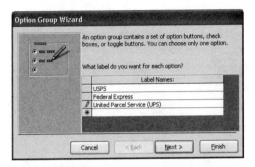

Figure 6.25 Enter a label for each option in the group.

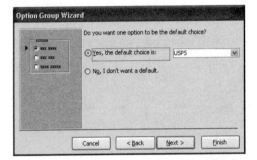

Figure 6.26 You can specify a *default choice* (a choice that is automatically selected for each new record).

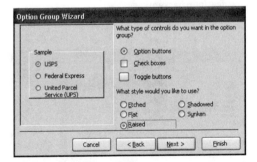

Figure 6.27 Select a control type and the manner in which it will be displayed.

Figure 6.28 This is an example of an option button option group.

Adding special controls

An Access field can be much more high tech than the rather ordinary "type your response" text box. You can create controls that display a scrolling value list, check boxes, or radio buttons from which the user can select a value or option. As an example, the following steps explain how to create an *option group* (a set of mutually exclusive choices presented as option/radio buttons, check boxes, or toggle buttons).

To create an option group:

1. Open the form in Design View.

2. Click the Option Group icon in the Toolbox, and click the form to set the control's position.

   The Option Group Wizard appears.

3. Enter the list of options in the Label Names boxes in the order that you want them to be listed (**Figure 6.25**). Click Next.

4. Click a radio button to indicate whether you want to set a default choice (**Figure 6.26**). If Yes, select the default from the drop-down list. Click Next to continue.

5. Each choice is assigned a value. You can either accept or modify the proposed values. Click Next to continue.

6. You can store the value for later use (in a macro, for example) or assign it to an existing field selected from the drop-down list. (Until you become a more advanced Access user, you will probably want to select the latter option.) Click Next.

7. On the next screen (**Figure 6.27**), select a control type and a display style. Click Next.

8. Enter a label for the new control, and click the Finish button.

   The new control appears on the form (**Figure 6.28**). Edit or resize it, as necessary.

Changing the Background

The form backgrounds provided with Access aren't particularly attractive. You can substitute a different background picture by changing the form's Picture property. For example, Web page backgrounds also make excellent form backgrounds.

To change the form background:

1. Open the form in Design View.

2. Select the form.

    You can click the *form selector* (the box where the two rulers intersect) or choose Form from the Objects toolbar menu.

3. Click the Properties toolbar icon, press [Alt][Enter], or choose View > Properties. The Form properties window opens.

4. On the Format tab (**Figure 6.29**), click the Picture property and then click the Build button to its right.

    The Insert Picture dialog box appears (**Figure 6.30**).

5. Select an image. Click OK (if required).

6. *Optional:* You can change the settings for the other Picture properties (Picture Type, Picture Size Mode, Picture Alignment, and Picture Tiling).

7. Close the Form properties window, and switch to Form View to see the new background.

✔ Tips

■ Light backgrounds tend to work best. Similarly, textures generally make more usable backgrounds than do photos (or any other complex image).

■ You can also change the background by choosing an AutoFormat setting. Open a form in Design View, click the AutoFormat toolbar icon, and choose a format (**Figure 6.31**).

Build button

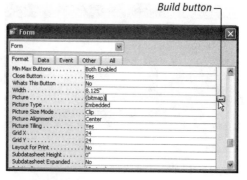

Figure 6.29 Click the Build button to select a background image from disk.

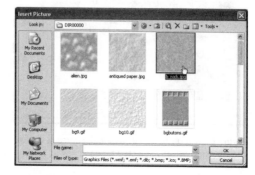

Figure 6.30 Select an image file from disk to serve as the new form background.

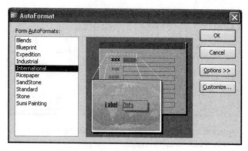

Figure 6.31 Another way to change the background is to select a new AutoFormat.

CHANGING THE BACKGROUND

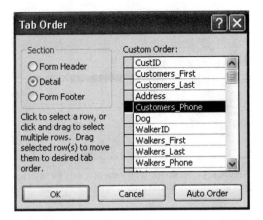

Figure 6.32 You can change a form's tab order in this dialog box.

Setting the Tab Order

A form's *tab order* (the order in which the cursor moves as you tab from field to field) depends on how the form was created. When Access generates a form, it sets a standard tab order: left-to-right and top-to-bottom. When you design a form manually, the tab order follows the order in which you place the fields.

An important step in finalizing any form is to ensure that the tab order works properly. If you've manually placed fields, moved fields, or added buttons to a form, you may need to change the tab order. Similarly, if you've created a form with logical divisions, you may want a tab order that reflects those divisions.

To set a custom tab order:

1. Select Forms in the Objects area of the Database window.

2. Select a form and click the Design toolbar icon.

3. Choose View > Tab Order.

   The Tab Order dialog box appears, open to the Detail Section of the form (**Figure 6.32**).

4. Click to select one or more contiguous fields and drag them to a new position in the tab order list. Repeat as necessary.

5. Click OK to set the new tab order.

✔ Tips

- To automatically set the tab order to the standard arrangement (left-to-right and top-to-bottom), click the Auto Order button.

- To prevent buttons from interfering with normal data entry, you may want to make them the final elements in the tab order. Alternatively, you can remove buttons (or any other element) from the tab order. Set the element's Tab Stop property (found on the Other tab) to No.

Tabbing Out of the Last Field

Normally, when you're in the last field on a form and press Tab, you tab to the first field of the next record. You can control the tabbing behavior of the last field by setting the form's Cycle property (found on the Other tab). Cycle property settings include:

- **All Records.** Tabbing out of the last field takes you to the first field of the following record (default setting).

- **Current Record.** Tabbing out of the last field takes you to the first field of the same record.

- **Current Page.** When working in a multi-page form, tabbing out of the last field on a page takes you to the first field on the same page.

Displaying Single or Continuous Forms

Normally, a form shows only a single record. To view other records, you use the navigation buttons at the bottom of the form. If you prefer, you can make any form display as a scrolling list. You can then move among records using the vertical scroll bar in addition to clicking the navigation buttons.

To show single or continuous forms:

1. Open the form in Design View.

2. Select the form.

   You can click the *form selector* (the box where the two rulers intersect) or choose Form from the Objects toolbar menu.

3. Click the Properties toolbar icon, press [Alt][Enter], or choose View > Properties.

   The Form properties window opens.

4. On the Format tab (**Figure 6.33**), set the Default View to Single Form or Continuous Forms.

5. Close the Form window and the form.

6. When prompted to save changes, click Yes.

   The form now uses its new default view (**Figure 6.34**).

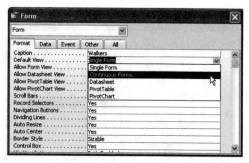

Figure 6.33 Set the Default View property by selecting an option from the drop-down list.

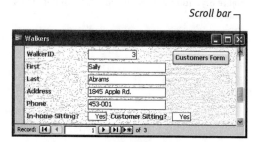

Figure 6.34 When Continuous Forms is selected, you can scroll from one record to the next.

CREATING RELATIONSHIPS

Microsoft Access is a *relational database program.* If you create or use databases that contain multiple tables, its reports, forms, and queries can draw information from the other tables. This is possible because the tables are *related* to one another.

For instance, suppose a Transportation Director has a database that she uses to manage the school's bus fleet. The Buses table contains route data for each bus. A Students table contains basic data for every student, such as name, age, sex, address, and phone number. By relating the two tables using the students' ID numbers, the Buses table can display the name, address, and phone number of every student on a given bus by entering nothing more than their ID numbers.

In this chapter, you will learn about the different kinds of relationships that Access supports, as well as how to define, modify, and print relationships.

Setting the Primary Key

In order to relate a pair of tables, you must have matching fields in the two tables. Unless a database will contain only one table or if a given table won't be related to other tables, every table should have a primary key. The *primary key* is a field that uniquely identifies each record.

When you create a new table, Access offers to define the primary key for you. An Access-generated primary key is a numbered integer sequence beginning with 1. However, if you already have an ID sequence as a field (such as a part, account, or Social Security number), you can specify that this existing field will be the primary key.

When you define a relationship, you match a primary key in one table to a field (called a *foreign key*) in another table. A foreign key can be any field; it isn't ever actually designated as a foreign key when defining fields for the table. The important thing is that the data in the foreign key field must provide a perfect match with the primary key in the main table. In the school database example, Bus Number could be the primary key in the Buses table, while Student ID served as primary key in the Students table. The relationship would be defined as the match between Student ID (the primary key in the Students table) and a similar field in the Buses table.

The method used to set a table's primary key—and the presented options for doing so—depends on the table creation method. If you neglect to set a primary key when you create a table, you can manually designate a primary key field at a more convenient time.

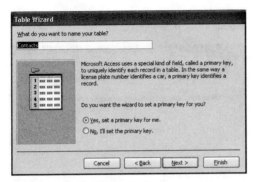

Figure 7.1 On this Table Wizard screen, you can select an existing field to use as the primary key or allow Access to create the primary key.

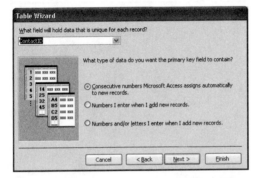

Figure 7.2 If you selected No in the previous screen, you are asked to select an existing field to serve as the primary key.

Figure 7.3 When you create a table by entering data, this dialog box appears after you close and save the table. Click Yes to instruct Access to create a primary key. To create your own primary key or do without one, click No.

To set the primary key when creating a table with the Table Wizard:

1. During the table creation process, a dialog box appears offering you the opportunity to create or designate a primary key (**Figure 7.1**).

2. *Select one of the following:*

   ▲ **Yes, set a primary key for me.** Let Access create a default primary key named ID.

   ▲ **No, I'll set the primary key.** Designate an existing field as the primary key. In the next screen (**Figure 7.2**), select the field that will serve as the primary key, and click a radio button to specify how the primary key for new records will be numbered.

To set the primary key when creating a table by entering data:

1. After entering the initial data to create the fields for the new table, click the table's close box.

2. Indicate that you want to save the table, and name it when prompted to do so.

   A new dialog box appears (**Figure 7.3**).

3. *Do one of the following:*

   ▲ Click Yes to allow Access to create the primary key. The field will be created and assigned the default name of ID. Numbers will be assigned to all existing records, beginning with 1.

   ▲ Click No to close the table without designating a primary key field. If you wish, you can later designate an existing field as the primary key or request that Access create one for you.

SETTING THE PRIMARY KEY

To manually set a primary key:

1. Open the table and switch to Design View.

2. If an appropriate field for the primary key doesn't exist, create the field now.

3. Click the field selector for the field that you want to make into the primary key or position the insertion mark in any part of the field.

4. Click the Primary Key toolbar icon or choose Edit > Primary Key.

   A key icon appears in the table, indicating that the selected field is now the primary key (**Figure 7.4**).

✔ Tips

- To change the primary key to a different field, select the correct field (as instructed in Step 3). Then click the Primary Key toolbar icon or choose Edit > Primary Key.

- To remove the primary key from a table, you must first delete any relationships that rely on the key (as explained later in this chapter). Then select the current primary key field and click the Primary Key toolbar icon to remove the field's primary key status.

- A primary key can also be a combination of several fields. For example, in a Contacts table, Last Name would generally be a poor choice for a primary key because of the high probability of duplication. However, combining Last Name and Birth Date is considerably more likely to result in unique combinations. To designate multiple fields as part of a primary key, press Ctrl as you select each field.

Primary Key indicator   Primary Key icon

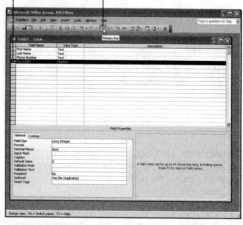

Figure 7.4 In Design View, you can easily designate, change, or remove a table's primary key.

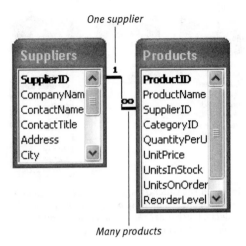

One supplier

Many products

Figure 7.5 An example of a one-to-many relationship based on the SupplierID field, as shown in the Relationships window.

Types of Relationships

A relationship is defined by specifying a pair of matching fields in two tables: a primary key field in one table and a foreign key (some field other than the primary key) in the second table. The fields do not have to share the same name (although they certainly can), but they *must* contain the same data. For example, in the school database mentioned earlier in this chapter, a relationship could be created by relating the ID field (primary key) in the Students table with the Student Number field in the Buses table.

Each relationship is of a particular type, depending on the nature of the related data in the two tables. Access enables you to create the following types of relationships:

♦ **One-to-many.** This is the most common type of relationship. Only one record in table A is related to multiple records in table B.

For example, in the Northwind sample database included with Access, there is a one-to-many relationship between the Suppliers and Products tables, formed by matching the SupplierID fields (**Figure 7.5**). In the Suppliers table, each supplier has a separate record identified by SupplierID (the primary key field). It wouldn't be surprising to see the same SupplierID many times, since one supplier might well be the provider of many products.

♦ **One-to-one.** In this type of relationship, there is a one-to-one correspondence between records in the two tables. Of course, you could also just include the fields from the second table in the first table, avoiding the necessity of a second table and a relationship. Reasons for creating a one-to-one relationship include the need to move seldom-used or sensitive data into a separate table.

◆ **Many-to-many.** In this type of relationship, any record in either table can potentially match multiple records in the other table. A many-to-many relationship cannot be created directly between a pair of tables. Instead, you must create an additional table called a *junction table* to which the relationships are made. The primary key in the junction table is a combination of the other two tables' foreign keys (**Figure 7.6**).

✔ Tip

■ When you define a new relationship, you don't have to tell Access its type. Access determines the relationship type by examining the data in the tables.

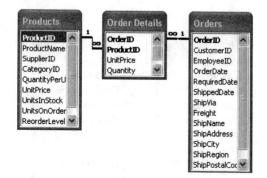

Figure 7.6 The Order Details junction table enables a many-to-many relationship between orders and products. (Each order can contain multiple products and each product can appear in multiple orders.)

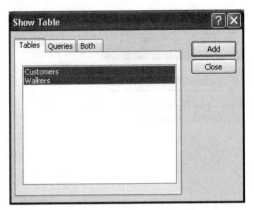

Figure 7.7 Select the tables/queries that you want to display in the Relationships window and click Add.

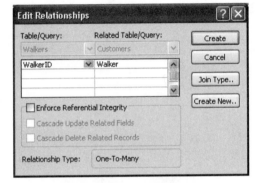

Figure 7.8 Set or view options for a relationship in the Edit Relationships dialog box.

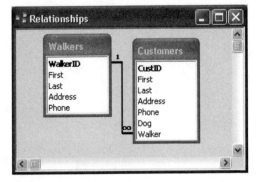

Figure 7.9 This one-to-many relationship pairs the WalkerID and Walker fields.

Defining Relationships

Relationships between tables are defined and modified in the Relationships window.

To create a relationship:

1. Choose Tools > Relationships.

   The Relationships window appears. If no relationships have been defined, the Show Table dialog box also appears (**Figure 7.7**). You can also choose Relationships > Show Table to open the dialog box.

2. Select the Tables and/or Queries that you wish to display, and click the Add button.

   The tables and/or queries appear in the Relationships window.

3. To dismiss the Show Table dialog box, click its close box or the Close button.

4. To create a relationship between tables or queries, drag a field from one table onto the matching field in another table.

   The Edit Relationships dialog box appears (**Figure 7.8**).

5. Examine the current settings for the relationship, make any needed changes, and click Create. (To learn about referential integrity, refer to the next section.)

   The Edits Relationship dialog box is dismissed and the new relationship is shown in the Relationships window (**Figure 7.9**).

6. Repeat Steps 4 and 5 as needed to create additional relationships.

7. Close the Relationships window and save (if prompted to do so).

✔ Tip

- To remove a table from the Relationships window, select the table and press (Del) (or choose Relationships > Hide Table). This has no effect on the actual table or relationships that depend on it.

To view or modify relationships:

1. Choose Tools > Relationships.

   The Relationships window appears (see Figure 7.9).

2. If the relationship that you want to change isn't displayed, choose Relationships > Show All or click the Show All Relationships toolbar icon (**Figure 7.10**).

3. Select the line for the relationship that you want to change.

   When a relationship line is selected, it appears darker or bolder than normal.

4. Choose Relationships > Edit Relationship or double-click the relationship line.

   The Edit Relationships dialog box appears (see Figure 7.8).

5. Make any necessary changes, and then click OK to close the dialog box.

6. Repeat Steps 3–5 for other relationships that you want to examine or change.

7. Close the Relationships window.

✔ Tips

■ To delete a relationship, select its line in the Relationships window and choose Edit > Delete or press [Del]. You can also delete a relationship by right-clicking the relationship line and choosing Delete from the pop-up menu that appears.

■ To view only the relationships for a single table, begin by removing everything from the Relationships window—click the Clear Layout toolbar icon or choose Edit > Clear Layout. Next, use the Show Table command to add the table to the Relationships window. Finally, click the Show Direct Relationships toolbar icon or choose Relationships > Show Direct.

■ To view all defined relationships, click the Show All Relationships toolbar icon or choose Relationships > Show All.

Show Direct Relationships

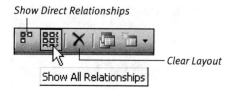

Clear Layout

Show All Relationships

Figure 7.10 The Relationships commands can be found on the toolbar.

Referential Integrity

Options in the Edit Relationships dialog box (see Figure 7.8) determine whether Access monitors the relationship and the actions you can perform on the related tables. When Enforce Referential Integrity has been enabled, the following restrictions are enforced:

◆ If a value doesn't exist in the primary key field of the main table, you can't enter it in the foreign key field of the related table.

◆ You can only delete a record from the primary table if there are no records that rely on it in the related table (unless you've also enabled Cascade Delete Related Fields). For example, you can't delete a record for a particular salesperson if there are still sales records for him or her in a related table.

◆ You can't change a primary key value if there are related records that rely on it (unless you've also enabled Cascade Update Related Fields).

To enforce referential integrity, the following must be true:

◆ The matching field in the primary table is either a primary key or has a *unique index;* that is, the Indexed property is set to Yes (No Duplicates).

◆ The related fields are of the same data type. However, an AutoNumber field can be related to a Number (Long Integer) field.

◆ The related tables are either in the same database or are linked Access tables.

When referential integrity is enforced, you can also enable cascading record updates and/or deletions. If you've enabled cascading updates and you change a primary key value in a record in the main table, Access also changes that value in all related records. With cascading deletions, deleting a record in the primary table causes the deletion of any related records in the related table.

Printing Relationships

Whether a database includes a handful of related tables or hundreds of them, you'll find that printing the Relationships window is an excellent way to document a database.

To print the Relationships window:

1. Choose Tools > Relationships.

   The Relationships window appears (see Figure 7.9).

2. Display the relationships to be printed. Show or hide tables, as necessary.

3. Choose File > Print Relationships.

   A print preview window appears (**Figure 7.11**).

4. Using the tools from the toolbar (such as the Zoom icon and drop-down list), examine the preview. If it's satisfactory, click the Print toolbar icon.

5. When you close the preview window, a dialog box appears, offering you the opportunity to save this as a named report. Do one of the following:

   ▲ Click No to close the window without saving.

   ▲ Click Yes to save it. Enter a name for the new report in the Save As dialog box (**Figure 7.12**).

✔ Tips

■ It isn't necessary to expand individual tables in the Relationships window—even if the field lists aren't fully displayed. During the Print Relationships procedure, tables are automatically expanded to show each complete field list.

■ Prior to printing, you can examine or change the default page setup options, such as margins, paper size, orientation, and which printer to use. Click the Setup toolbar icon to view or set these options (**Figure 7.13**).

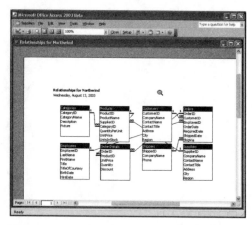

Figure 7.11 A preview of the relationships printout is presented in a new window.

Figure 7.12 To save the current Relationships window as a report, name it and click OK.

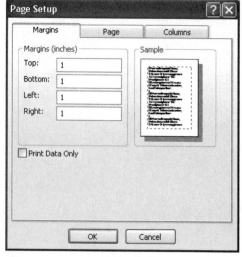

Figure 7.13 You can change layout and print settings on the tabs of the Page Setup dialog box.

DATA ENTRY AND EDITING

After spending the previous seven chapters learning to create and customize databases, you should be champing at the bit to begin entering and editing data; that is, actually *using* your databases.

In this chapter, you'll learn to do the following:

◆ Create new records and delete existing records that are no longer needed

◆ Navigate between records in a datasheet or a form

◆ Enter new data and edit existing data

◆ Use the Find and Replace commands to locate particular data and—optionally—replace it with other data

◆ Use the Spelling tool to perform spell checks on selected text, fields, or records

Adding New Records

When you're ready to enter new data into a database, you begin by creating a new record. Access provides several ways to create records. Use whichever method(s) you find convenient.

To create a new record:

◆ *Do one of the following:*

▲ Choose Insert > New Record (or press Ctrl +).

▲ Click the New Record toolbar icon (**Figure 8.1**).

▲ Click the New Record navigation button at the bottom of the current form or datasheet (**Figure 8.2**).

▲ On a datasheet, click anywhere within (or tab into) the blank record at the bottom of the table, and enter your data (**Figure 8.3**).

✔ Tip

■ If you don't enter any data into a new record, Access discards it.

Figure 8.1 Click the New Record toolbar icon.

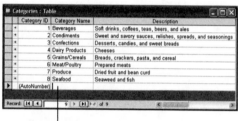

Figure 8.2 Or you can click this navigation button to create a new record.

Category ID	Category Name	Description
1	Beverages	Soft drinks, coffees, teas, beers, and ales
2	Condiments	Sweet and savory sauces, relishes, spreads, and seasonings
3	Confections	Desserts, candies, and sweet breads
4	Dairy Products	Cheeses
5	Grains/Cereals	Breads, crackers, pasta, and cereal
6	Meat/Poultry	Prepared meats
7	Produce	Dried fruit and bean curd
8	Seafood	Seaweed and fish
(AutoNumber)		

New record

Figure 8.3 In Datasheet View, the blank record at the bottom represents a new record.

Figure 8.4 The Delete Record toolbar icon.

Record selector

Figure 8.5 When an entire record is selected, you can right-click anywhere within it and choose Delete Record from the pop-up menu. (Regardless of what is selected, you can *always* right-click the record selector.)

Figure 8.6 A warning dialog appears whenever you attempt to delete one or more records.

Deleting Records

When one or more records are no longer needed (such as a shipper you don't use or a contact that you don't want to track anymore), you can delete them. Since there is no Undo command for record deletions, you should make them carefully and also maintain backups of all important data.

To delete a single record:

1. Open the appropriate datasheet, form, or query result.

2. Select the record to be deleted (in the datasheet, subdatasheet, form, or subform) by doing one of the following:

   ▲ In a datasheet or query result, move the cursor/insertion point into any field of the record or click the record selector to select the entire record.

   ▲ In a form, display the record that you want to delete.

3. *Do one of the following:*

   ▲ Click the Delete Record toolbar icon (**Figure 8.4**).

   ▲ Choose Edit > Delete Record.

   ▲ If an entire record in a datasheet or query result is selected, you can also choose Edit > Delete, press Del, or right-click anywhere within the record and choose Delete Record from the pop-up menu (**Figure 8.5**).

   A warning dialog box appears (**Figure 8.6**).

4. Click Yes to complete the deletion, or click No to cancel it.

To delete multiple records:

1. Open the appropriate datasheet, form, or query result.

2. Select the contiguous range of records to be deleted (in the datasheet, subdatasheet, form, or subform) by doing one of the following:

   ▲ In a datasheet, subdatasheet, subform, or query result, click the record selector of the first record and then—while holding down [Shift]—click the record selector of the final record. Or click the record selector of the first record, and then drag-select the additional records.

   ▲ In a datasheet, subdatasheet, form, subform, query result, or filtered datasheet or form, choose Edit > Select All Records or press [Ctrl][A].

3. Click the Delete Record toolbar icon (see Figure 8.4), or choose Edit > Delete Record. A warning dialog box appears (see Figure 8.6).

4. Click Yes to complete the deletion, or click No to cancel it.

✔ Tips

■ Another way to select a record in a datasheet is to click or tab into in any of its fields and choose Edit > Select Record.

■ In a database with related tables, deleting a record on the "one" side of a one-to-many relationship may also result in the deletion of related records (as shown in Figure 8.6). For instance, deleting a customer record may also delete the customer's invoices, depending on whether cascading deletes has been enabled. See Chapter 7 for information on cascading deletes.

■ Some deletions are not allowed. You cannot delete a record that is required by other tables, for example.

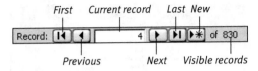

Figure 8.7 Navigation buttons are displayed at the bottoms of datasheets and forms.

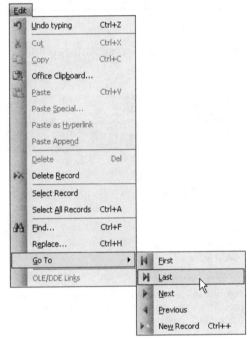

Figure 8.8 Navigation commands can also be found in the Edit > Go To submenu.

Table 8.1

Record Navigation Keyboard Shortcuts		
KEYSTROKE	MODE	EFFECT
[Pg Dn] or [Pg Up]	Form	Next or previous record
[↓] or [↑]	Datasheet	Next or previous record
[Pg Dn] or [Pg Up]	Datasheet	Down/up one screen full of records
[Ctrl][↑] or [Ctrl][↓]	Form or Datasheet	First or last record in the table

Navigating Among Records

Whether you're creating and editing records or just viewing data, it's important to know how to move from one record to another. Although the navigation buttons (**Figure 8.7**) at the bottom of a datasheet or form serve as the primary means of between-record navigation, there are other methods, too.

To move between records:

1. Open a datasheet, form, or query result.

2. Using the navigation buttons, you can do the following:
   ▲ Go to the first or last record in the current datasheet or form.
   ▲ Go to the previous or next record.
   ▲ Go to a specific record by typing its number in the text box and pressing [Tab], [Return], or [Enter].

✔ Tips

■ All navigation is relative to the current sort order of the active datasheet or form.

■ You can also use your keyboard's navigation keys to move among the records. The most useful commands are shown in **Table 8.1**. The commands also work in subdatasheets and subforms.

■ Another way to navigate among records is by choosing commands from the Edit > Go To submenu (**Figure 8.8**).

■ In a datasheet, if you tab past the last field of a record or press [Shift][Tab] when in the first field, you move to the next or previous record, respectively.

■ To quickly select the record number box (to go to a record by number), press [F5].

Entering and Editing Data

Unless you're using a static database (for viewing data only), you'll probably spend a considerable amount of time entering new data and editing existing data.

Entering text

In most databases, the majority of data is text. Procedures for entering other types of data are discussed later in this section.

To enter text data into a record:

1. Open the appropriate datasheet or form.

2. *Do one of the following:*
   ▲ Create a new record to receive the data.
   ▲ Click in the field of an existing record where you want to begin entering data.

3. In each field, enter data by typing (**Figure 8.9**), clicking a check box or option button, or selecting a value from a drop-down list.

4. To move to the next field, press Tab. To move to the previous field, press Shift Tab.

5. Repeat Steps 3 and 4 for each field in which you want to enter data.

   If you switch records (or close the datasheet or form), Access saves the changes.

✔ Tips

■ You can go directly to any field in the current record by clicking in the field or by choosing the field name's from the Go To Field drop-down list in the Formatting (Datasheet) toolbar (**Figure 8.10**). To display the toolbar, choose View > Toolbars > Formatting (Datasheet).

■ You can also enter and edit related data in a subdatasheet or subform. To expose a record's subdatasheet (**Figure 8.11**), click its *expand indicator* (the + symbol).

■ Another way to create new records is to choose Records > Data Entry.

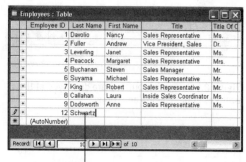

New data

Figure 8.9 Typing new data into a datasheet field.

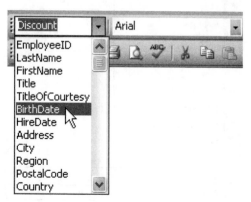

Figure 8.10 You can select a field to go to in the current record from this drop-down list on the Formatting (Datasheet) toolbar.

Expand indicator

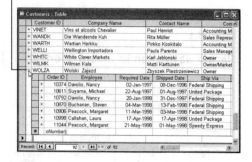

Figure 8.11 To enter or edit data in a subdatasheet, click its expand indicator.

Entering numbers, dates, times

For the most part, entering data into a Number, Currency, or Date/Time field is straightforward. Here are a few helpful facts:

◆ When entering data in a Number or Currency field, you only need to type the numbers (with a decimal place and sign, if necessary), such as *12.45* or *-1500*. Although Access will accept other characters in a number (such as a dollar sign or commas), they aren't required.

◆ To indicate a negative number, precede it with a minus sign or surround the number with parentheses, such as *(459)*.

◆ When typing a date, almost any format will suffice. For example, all of these entries are equivalent: *12/1/1990; 12-01-90; Dec 1, 1990; December 1, 1990;* and *1-dec-90*.

◆ When entering the year portion of a date using only two digits, Access interprets the numbers 00–29 as being 2000–2029. All other two-digit years are assumed to be in the 1900s. (Note that you can always enter a year as a 4-digit number to avoid any potential confusion.)

◆ If you omit the year portion of a date (as in *12/15*), Access assumes that you mean the current year.

◆ Like dates, times can be entered in several ways. You can enter hours, minutes, and—optionally—seconds, followed by an AM or PM designation. Or you can enter time in military format. All of these examples are equivalent: *1:35p, 1:35 PM, 1:35:00 PM,* and *13:35*.

◆ If you omit the AM or PM prefix from a time, entries between 0 and 11:59 are interpreted as AM times.

ENTERING AND EDITING DATA

Entering hyperlinks

Hyperlink fields (**Figure 8.12**) contain clickable links to Web sites, FTP sites (for downloading and/or uploading data), email addresses (to generate messages to a person or company), or data files on your computer.

At a minimum, a hyperlink must contain a valid address. **Table 8.2** shows examples of the most common types of addresses. A link can optionally contain *display text* (text that appears in the field instead of the address), a subaddress, and a ScreenTip, as follows:

displaytext#address#subaddress#screentip

Skipped components are represented by the # symbol. For instance, this hyperlink:

#http://www.hotmail.com##Hotmail site

would show *http://www.hotmail.com* as the link (since display text wasn't included) and display *Hotmail site* as the ScreenTip when you rest the cursor over the link. If a ScreenTip is omitted, the link text becomes the ScreenTip.

Hyperlinks can be created by typing, by pasting a copied link (an email address from a received message, for example), by using drag and drop (such as dragging an address from the Address box in Internet Explorer), or by using the Insert > Hyperlink command.

To add a link using Insert > Hyperlink:

1. Open the appropriate datasheet or form and position the insertion point in the Hyperlink field that will receive the link.

2. Choose Insert > Hyperlink or press ⌃Ctrl ⌃K. The Insert Hyperlink dialog box appears (**Figure 8.13**).

3. Click a Link to: icon to specify the type of link that you want to create.

Figure 8.12 Here are some examples of clickable hyperlinks.

Link to icons

Figure 8.13 If you aren't comfortable typing hyperlinks, you can select a link item in this dialog box.

Table 8.2

Hyperlink Examples

Address Type	Example
Web site	http://www.siliconwasteland.com
Email address	mailto:roadrunner12@netzone.net
FTP site	ftp://ftp.microsoft.com
Local document	C:\Documents\mobile.txt

Figure 8.14 Enter the optional ScreenTip text in this dialog box.

Figure 8.15 Specify an email address and optional Subject text in this dialog box.

4. If linking to a file on your computer, do the following:
   ▲ Navigate to the file's location on disk and select its name from the file list. To select from all recently opened files, click the Recent Files icon.
   ▲ *Optional:* Edit the text in the Text to display box.
   ▲ *Optional:* To create a pop-up ScreenTip (**Figure 8.14**), click the ScreenTip button, enter the tip text, and click OK.

5. If linking to a Web page, do one of the following:
   ▲ Type or paste the address into the Address text box.
   ▲ Click the Browsed Pages icon to select from pages that you recently visited in your browser.
   ▲ Click the down arrow at the right end of the Address box to view another list of recently visited pages.
   ▲ Click the Browse the Web icon. Your browser opens. Display the Web page to which you want to link, and then return to Access. The address and display text are automatically transferred.
   You can edit the display text and create a ScreenTip, if you wish.

6. If linking to an email address (**Figure 8.15**), type or paste it into the E-mail address text box. If you like, you can also specify the Subject text, edit the display text, and create a ScreenTip.

7. Click OK.

✔ Tips

■ To delete a hyperlink, tab into the field and press (Del) or (Backspace).

■ A ScreenTip can be extremely helpful for identifying a Web page. In many cases, a page's address may not give the slightest clue concerning its contents.

Inserting pictures and OLE objects

The procedure for inserting a picture (as well as any other OLE object) into a field is very different from that of entering text.

To insert a picture into an OLE Object field:

1. Open the appropriate datasheet or form.

2. *Do one of the following:*
   - ▲ Select the field and choose Insert Object.
   - ▲ Right-click the field and choose Insert Object from the pop-up menu.

   A dialog box appears (**Figure 8.16**).

3. *Do one of the following:*
   - ▲ To create a new object, click Create New, select an object type from the list, and click OK. The chosen program launches. Create the object or image, and close its window. You return to Access.
   - ▲ To insert an image from an existing file, click Create from File, and click OK. In the new dialog box (**Figure 8.17**), select a file by clicking Browse. (By default, a static copy of the image will be embedded in the field. To create a link to the file enabling changes to it to be automatically displayed, click the Link check box.) In the Browse dialog box (**Figure 8.18**), select an image or other object to insert, and click OK. Click OK to insert the image.

   The image or object is inserted into the field.

✔ Tips

- ■ If an inserted object cannot be displayed, Access shows only its filename. To view the object in the program in which it was created, double-click the filename.

- ■ You can display a clickable icon in the field rather than the actual object by clicking the Display as Icon check box (see Figures 8.16 and 8.17).

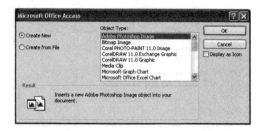

Figure 8.16 You can either create a new OLE object in another application program (such as Adobe Photoshop) or insert one from an existing file.

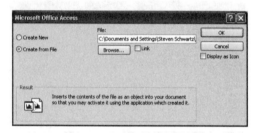

Figure 8.17 Click Browse to select an OLE object file stored on disk.

Selected file   *Image preview*

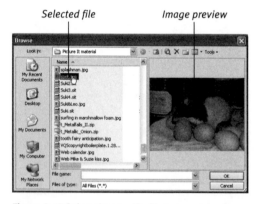

Figure 8.18 Select the specific file to insert. Image files such as this one may display a preview.

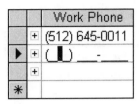

Figure 8.19 Click in a field that is formatted with an input mask to view the mask.

Click to view the list

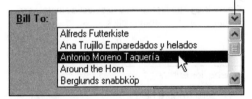

Figure 8.20 Click the down-arrow to view the choices in a value list that's attached to a field.

Figure 8.21 This set of radio or option buttons is an example of an *option group*.

Data entry tips and considerations

Here's some additional information that you'll find helpful when entering data.

◆ What you type and how the data in a given field is displayed aren't necessarily the same thing. Different date, time, and number display formats can be specified, for example. When you enter data in such a field, it is automatically reformatted.

◆ Similarly, a field can have an *input mask* that controls the manner in which data is entered and displayed. An input mask for a phone number might ignore all input except numbers and automatically format the data as *(xxx) xxx-xxxx*. Input masks can be present in forms or datasheets (**Figure 8.19**).

◆ The maximum number of characters allowed in a given field is set in its Field Size property. When entering data, you will be stopped if you try to enter additional characters.

◆ Some fields may have a default value that is automatically entered whenever you create a new record. The default value for Country might be *USA,* for example. To replace the default value for a given record, just type over it with the new entry.

◆ Some fields present a drop-down list of values (**Figure 8.20**). Use the mouse to select a value or type the first few letters to select the closest match.

◆ If a field is presented as a series of mutually exclusive check boxes, radio/option buttons (**Figure 8.21**), or toggle buttons, you can press → or ← to select an item. Of course, you can also use the mouse to click the desired option.

◆ Check boxes and option buttons that *aren't* in an option group can be toggled between selected/unselected by pressing Spacebar.

Editing existing data

The procedures for editing data are similar (but not identical) to the ones you're already familiar with in other programs.

To edit existing data:

1. Open the appropriate datasheet or form.

2. Navigate to the record you want to edit.

   You can also go to the record by issuing a Find command, as explained later in this chapter.

3. Click to set the insertion point in the field you wish to edit.

4. *Do one of the following:*

   ▲ To add additional text to the field, click to position the insertion point and then type the text.

   ▲ To delete a character to the left of the insertion point or to delete selected text, press [Backspace].

   ▲ To replace the entire contents of the field, move the cursor over the left edge of the field. When it changes to a plus symbol (**Figure 8.22**), click once to select the entire field. Type the new text, replacing the old data.

   ▲ To select a single word, double-click the word (**Figure 8.23**).

   ▲ To delete an OLE object in a field, click to select the field and press [Backspace]. (Note that it isn't necessary to delete an object before replacing it with another one. Simply issue the Insert > Object command and choose the new object.)

   When you switch to another record or close the current datasheet or form, Access saves the changes to the record.

✔ Tip

■ To specify the cursor's behavior when entering a field (**Figure 8.24**), choose Tools > Options, and click the Keyboard tab.

Plus cursor

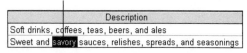

Figure 8.22 Click the left edge of any field to select its entire contents.

Selected word

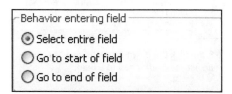

Figure 8.23 The fastest way to select a single word within a field is to double-click it.

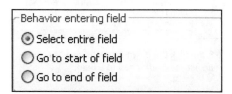

Figure 8.24 This option determines what happens when you tab into a field that contains data.

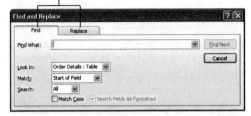

Figure 8.25 The Find toolbar icon.

Find and Replace tabs

Figure 8.26 You can perform a Find or a Find/Replace in this dialog box. To switch from one to the other, click the appropriate tab at the top of the dialog box.

Using Find and Replace

Using the Find and Replace commands, you can easily locate records that you want to view or edit. Find/Replace searches only the current table and can do any of the following:

◆ Locate a text string in a specific field or anywhere in the table

◆ Return matches found only at the start of a field, anywhere within the field, or only matches for an entire field

◆ From the current cursor position, search up, down, or the entire table

◆ Match or ignore letter case

◆ Search based on display format or on the stored value (ignoring the format)

◆ Perform a global replacement or replace data on a case-by-case basis

To perform a Find:

1. Open the appropriate datasheet or form.

2. To search a particular field, position the insertion point in that field.

   If you will be searching the entire table, the insertion point's location is irrelevant.

3. *Do one of the following:*

   ▲ Click the Find toolbar icon (**Figure 8.25**).

   ▲ Choose Edit > Find (or press Ctrl F).

   ▲ Choose Edit > Replace (or press Ctrl H).

   The Find and Replace dialog box appears (**Figure 8.26**). Click the Find tab, if needed.

4. Enter a search string in the Find What box.

   To reuse a previously entered string, click the down arrow at the right side of the Find What box and select the string.

5. Specify where to search (the current field or the entire table) by selecting an option from the Look In drop-down list.

   continues on next page

6. Select a matching criterion from the Match drop-down list: Any Part of Field, Whole Field, or Start of Field.

7. Select a search direction from the Search drop-down list: Up or Down (search only records above or below the current record), or All (search the entire table, form, sub-datasheet, or subform).

8. *Optional:* To restrict matches to those that have the same letter case (so the search string *Apple* would not find *apple*), click the Match Case check box.

9. *Optional:* To restrict matches to those that have the same display format, click the Search Fields As Formatted check box.

10. Click the Find Next button.

The first match (if there is one) is highlighted or its record is selected (**Figure 8.27**).

11. To search for additional matches, click Find Next again.

When no additional matches are found, a dialog box appears (**Figure 8.28**). Click OK to dismiss it.

To perform a Replace:

1. Perform Steps 1–9 of the previous step list.

2. Enter a replacement text string or number in the Replace With text box (**Figure 8.29**).

To reuse a previously entered string, click the down-arrow at the right side of the Replace With box and select the string.

3. *Do one of the following:*

▲ To automatically replace all matches with the replacement text string or number, click Replace All.

▲ To view each match and decide whether to replace it on a case-by-case basis, click the Find Next button. To replace an occurrence, click Replace. To skip an occurrence, click Find Next.

Match

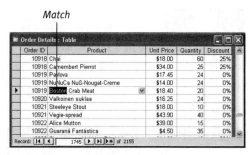

Figure 8.27 Access identifies a match by highlighting the match string or the record in which it is found.

Figure 8.28 This dialog box appears at the conclusion of a Find or Replace.

Figure 8.29 This example will search the Company Name field for instances where *Microsoft* is the entire field contents and replace it with *Microsoft Corporation*.

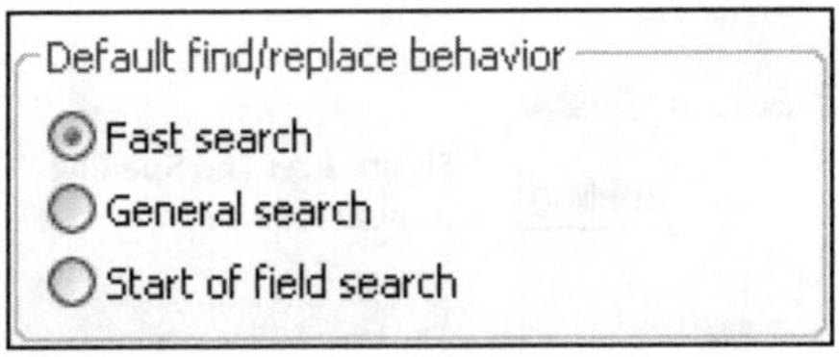

Figure 8.30 In order, these options search the current field and match the whole field, search all fields and match any part, and search the current field and match the beginning characters.

✔ Tips

- To halt a Find or Replace, click Cancel.

- To search for a word or number that's already in a record, start by selecting the word or number. Access will propose the selected text or number as the Find What string.

- Find/Replace can also be performed in a subdatasheet or subform. Use the same procedure, but begin with the insertion point in a subdatasheet or subform field.

- When searching a subdatasheet, only the current one is examined. Unless the intent is to restrict the Find/Replace to only the current record, it may be more profitable to search the related table directly.

- When checked, the Search Fields As Formatted check box requires that you type the search string so that it matches the display format. Depending on the field you're searching, you may want to disable this option. In a Date field, for example, you could then enter *12/8/68* or *Dec 8, 1968* to find *08-Dec-1968*.

- The Search Fields As Formatted option can give unexpected results. If Access is unable to find the string for which you're searching, try toggling the state of the check box.

- You can specify the default Find behavior by choosing Tools > Options. In the Options dialog box, click the Edit/Find tab (**Figure 8.30**).

Checking Spelling

Whether you need serious assistance with your spelling or just want Access to help you catch an occasional typo, you can use the Spelling command to find and correct your mistakes.

To check spelling in a datasheet or query result:

1. Open the datasheet or query result.

2. *Do one of the following:*
   ▲ To check specific text in a single field of one record, select the text.
   ▲ To check text in multiple, contiguous fields of one record, drag-select through the text in those fields.
   ▲ To check the text of a single field for all the records, click the field's heading.
   ▲ To check the text in multiple, contiguous fields for all records, click the first field heading and [Shift]-click the final heading.
   ▲ To check all text in a singe record, click the record selector.
   ▲ To check all text in multiple, contiguous records, click the top record selector and then drag-select the additional records.
   ▲ To check all text in all records, choose Edit > Select All Records or press [Ctrl][A].
   ▲ To check the remaining text in the table (starting from the field where the insertion point is located), set the insertion point in a particular field and record.

3. Click the Spelling toolbar icon (**Figure 8.31**), choose Tools > Spelling, or press [F7]. The Spelling dialog box appears (**Figure 8.32**), displaying the first suspect word.

4. If the correct language dictionary isn't shown, select it from the Dictionary Language drop-down list.

Spelling

Figure 8.31 The Spelling toolbar icon.

Suspect word

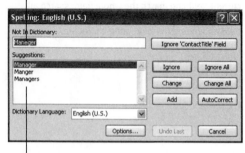

Possible replacements

Figure 8.32 Spell checks are performed in this dialog box.

5. For each suspect word, do one of the following:

▲ To ignore the current word and skip the indicated field for the remainder of the spell check, click Ignore *'field name'* Field.

▲ To ignore only this instance of the suspect word, click Ignore.

▲ To ignore this and every other instance of the suspect word, click Ignore All.

▲ To change this instance of the suspect word to the word selected in the Suggestions list, click Change. (You can also edit the text in the Not In Dictionary text box and click Change.)

▲ To change all instances of the suspect word to the word selected in the Suggestions list, click Change All. (You can also edit the text in the Not In Dictionary text box and click Change All.)

▲ To accept the suspect word as spelled correctly and add its spelling to the custom dictionary, click Add.

▲ If this is a word that you frequently misspell *the same way,* select the correct spelling in the Suggestions list or correct it in the Not in Dictionary text box, and then click AutoCorrect. Doing so adds the word to Office's AutoCorrect list, enabling it to be automatically corrected for you during data entry.

▲ To immediately end the spelling check, click Cancel.

6. Repeat Step 5 for each additional suspect word. When the spelling check has been completed, a dialog box appears. Click OK.

CHECKING SPELLING

✔ Tips

- Spell checking in a form is essentially the same as in a datasheet. To restrict the spell check to the current record, choose Edit > Select Record.

- To initiate a spell check for an entire datasheet, form, or query, select the object in the Database window. Then click the Spelling toolbar icon, choose Tools > Spelling, or press F7.

- To set spell checking preferences (**Figure 8.33**), click the Options button in the Spelling dialog box (see Figure 8.32), or choose Tools > Options and click the Spelling tab. See Chapter 20 for details.

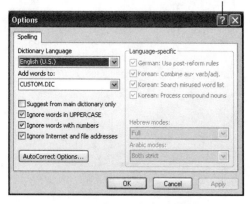

Figure 8.33 You can customize the way a spell check is performed by setting options in this dialog box. To learn the meaning of any option, click the ? and then click the option for which you want an explanation.

SORTING RECORDS

Unless a database is time- or transaction-based (such as an accounting system), the order in which you enter new records is seldom meaningful. As a result, viewing the data in original record order generally isn't very useful.

To view your records in an order that *is* meaningful, you can sort them in ascending or descending order, based on the values in one or more fields. In a student record database, for example, you might sort according to Student ID, or you could sort on Last Name and then First Name. The specific sort you request will depend on the order in which you want to view the data.

Records can be sorted in datasheet or form view. In addition, you can also specify a sort order for any query, report, PivotTable, or PivotChart. In a datasheet, form, query, or report, sorts can be performed on any data type except an OLE object.

The focus of this chapter is on sorting as an aid to viewing records in a datasheet or form. Sorting in other instances (queries, reports, PivotTables, and PivotCharts) will be discussed in the chapters devoted to those topics.

About Sorting in Access

In Access, there are two types of sorts: simple and complex. In a *simple sort*, all records are arranged in either ascending or descending order based on the contents of one or multiple sort fields. A *complex sort* mixes both ascending and descending sort fields.

Sorts are saved with the object with which they're associated. For example, if you sort using a particular form, the next time you open the form, its most recent sort will still be in effect. If you later create a new object based on a sorted object (such as a form, datasheet, query, or report), the new object will inherit the original object's sort order. You can restore a table's default sort order (sorted by its primary key) by choosing Records > Remove Filter/Sort (**Figure 9.1**).

There are several limitations related to sorting:

◆ When viewing records in a form, you can sort on only one field at a time.

◆ When working in a datasheet, you can sort on multiple fields. However, all sort fields must be *contiguous*—they will be performed from left to right. And you cannot mix ascending and descending sorts.

◆ You must perform a complex sort if you wish to mix ascending and descending sorts. Access provides the Advanced Filter/Sort window in which to design and execute complex sorts (see "Complex Sorts," later in this chapter). A complex sort can also be created when designing a new report or query in Design view.

◆ When sorting a Text field that contains numeric data, Access sorts the numeric data as though it were text. The records are sorted based on the first digit in the field, and the remaining digits are used to break ties. For instance, an ascending sort would result in this data arrangement: 2307, 317, 6, and 804.

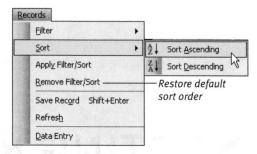

Figure 9.1 The Records menu contains all of the Sort commands, including the ability to remove a sort.

✔ Tip

■ When a sort field is empty for one or more records, the records with blanks for the field will appear first in an ascending sort.

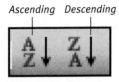

Ascending *Descending*

Figure 9.2 One way to execute a sort is to select a field and then click a Sort toolbar icon.

Selected sort field

Sort commands

Figure 9.3 You can right-click a field and then choose a Sort command from this pop-up menu.

Sorting When Using a Form

When working with a form, you can sort the records by any individual field.

To sort records when using a form:

1. In the Database window, click the Forms object and then double-click the form that you want to open.

   The form opens in its own window.

2. Click or tab into the field by which you want to sort.

3. *Do one of the following:*
   - ▲ Click the Sort Ascending or Sort Descending toolbar icon (**Figure 9.2**).
   - ▲ Choose Records > Sort > Sort Ascending or Records > Sort > Sort Descending.
   - ▲ Right-click the sort field. Choose Sort Ascending or Sort Descending from the pop-up menu that appears (**Figure 9.3**).

   The database is sorted per your instructions and the first record in the new sort order is displayed.

4. If you later wish to restore the default sort order (by the primary key field), choose Records > Remove Filter/Sort.

   You can also accomplish this by right-clicking any field and choosing Remove Filter/Sort from the pop-up menu that appears (see Figure 9.3).

5. *Optional:* To save the current sort order, save the form by choosing File > Save, pressing Ctrl S, or clicking the Save toolbar icon.

✔ Tip

- ■ It doesn't matter which record you're currently viewing when you perform a sort.

SORTING WHEN USING A FORM

103

Sorting a Datasheet

Sorting a datasheet by a single field is easier than sorting by multiple fields. Single-field sorts in a datasheet are no more difficult than performing the same action within a form.

To sort a datasheet on a single field:

1. In the Database window (**Figure 9.4**), click the Tables object and then double-click the table that you want to open.

   The table opens in its own window.

2. Click or tab into the field on which you want to sort.

3. *Do one of the following:*

   ▲ Click the Sort Ascending or Sort Descending toolbar icon (see Figure 9.2).

   ▲ Choose Records > Sort > Sort Ascending or Records > Sort > Sort Descending.

   ▲ Right-click the sort field. Choose Sort Ascending or Sort Descending from the pop-up menu that appears (see Figure 9.3).

   The database is sorted per your instructions.

4. If you later wish to restore the default sort order (by the primary key field), choose Records > Remove Filter/Sort.

   You can also accomplish this by right-clicking any field and choosing Remove Filter/Sort from the pop-up menu that appears (see Figure 9.3).

5. *Optional:* To save the current sort order, save the form by choosing File > Save, pressing Ctrl S, or clicking the Save toolbar icon.

Tables object   Defined Tables

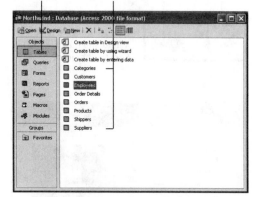

Figure 9.4 Select the data table with which you want to work.

Sorting Subforms and Subdatasheets

Forms and datasheets can contain *subforms* and *subdatasheets* (related data that is nested within a form or datasheet). To sort data within a subform or subdatasheet, you use the same methods that you use to sort forms and datasheets.

You can sort on any single field in a subform. Select the field, and issue a Sort Ascending or Sort Descending command.

You can sort on one or several adjacent fields in a subdatasheet. Display the subdatasheet for any record by clicking its *expand indicator* (the + icon), rearrange the fields as needed, select the sort fields, and then issue the desired Sort command.

Selected columns

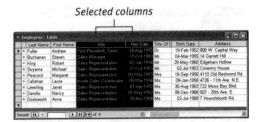

Figure 9.5 Select the contiguous columns by which you want to sort.

Hidden columns

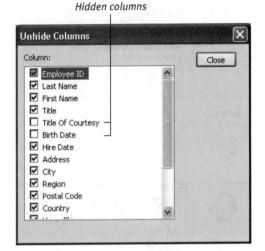

Figure 9.6 The hidden columns in the current datasheet are the ones without checkmarks. Click their entries to unhide them.

✔ Tip

■ If the columns are in the correct order but aren't contiguous, it may not be necessary to physically rearrange them. Instead, you can simply *hide* the unwanted columns and—after performing the sort—unhide them. To hide columns, select their headers and choose Format > Hide Columns. To display the hidden columns, choose Format > Unhide Columns. In the Unhide Columns dialog box (**Figure 9.6**), check each field that you want to reveal.

To sort a datasheet on multiple fields:

1. In the Database window (see Figure 9.4), click the Tables object and then double-click the table that you want to open.

   The table opens in its own window.

2. Rearrange the columns as necessary by dragging their headers left or right to new positions in the datasheet.

   All columns to be used as sort fields must be next to one another. Remember that the sorts will be performed on the leftmost field first and then proceed to the right through the remaining sort fields.

3. Select the sort fields by clicking in the leftmost column and then Shift-clicking in the rightmost column (**Figure 9.5**).

   You can select the sort fields within any single record by selecting the fields' column headers.

4. *Do one of the following:*

   ▲ Click the Sort Ascending or Sort Descending toolbar icon (see Figure 9.2).

   ▲ Choose Records > Sort > Sort Ascending or Records > Sort > Sort Descending.

   ▲ Right-click the sort field (while still holding down the Shift key). Choose Sort Ascending or Sort Descending from the pop-up menu that appears (see Figure 9.3).

   The database is sorted per your instructions.

5. If you later wish to restore the default sort order (by the primary key field), choose Records > Remove Filter/Sort.

   You can also accomplish this by right-clicking any field and choosing Remove Filter/Sort from the pop-up menu that appears (see Figure 9.3).

6. *Optional:* To save the current sort order, save the form by choosing File > Save, pressing Ctrl S, or clicking the Save toolbar icon.

Complex Sorts

Simple sorts are excellent when—in fact—they are easy to execute, as when sorting by a single field in a datasheet or form. Multi-field sorts in a datasheet, however, are seldom easy. They often necessitate rearranging the datasheet. To avoid the inconvenience of coaxing a simple sort to do your bidding, you can use the Advanced Filter/Sort window to create complex, multi-field sorts. Besides being the only way to mix ascending and descending sort fields, complex sorts allow you to keep the datasheet columns in their original positions.

To perform a complex sort:

1. In the Database window (see Figure 9.4), open the table (datasheet) or form that you want to view.

2. Choose Records > Filter > Advanced Filter/Sort.
   The Filter window appears (**Figure 9.7**),

3. Sorts in the Filter window are performed from left to right. Select the first sort field from the Field drop-down list, and then select Ascending or Descending from the Sort drop-down list (**Figure 9.8**).

4. To sort on additional fields, repeat Step 3 as many times as necessary.

5. To execute the sort(s), click the Apply Filter toolbar (**Figure 9.9**) or choose Filter > Apply Filter/Sort.
   The Filter window closes and the datasheet or form reappears, sorted per your instructions.

✔ Tips

- The Criteria and the Or boxes in the Filter window are for specifying record selection (filtering) criteria. To learn about filtering, see Chapter 10.

- You use this same procedure to specify a complex sort as part of a query.

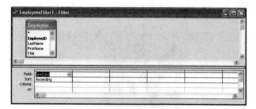

Figure 9.7 You can use the Filter window to quickly design a multi-field sort.

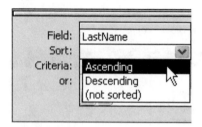

Figure 9.8 When you click in the Field and Sort boxes, you can select a sort field and a sort order from drop-down lists.

Figure 9.9 To apply your sort instructions to the current table, form, or query, click the Apply Filter toolbar icon.

10

FILTERING DATA

When browsing through records in a datasheet or form, it's often helpful to be able to focus on a particular group of records. Rather than browsing an entire table, you might want to view only female employees, recipes that contain beef as the main ingredient, or unpaid invoices that are more than 30 days past due.

Access provides two features for selecting record subsets: filters and queries. (Queries— the more complex of the two—are discussed separately in Chapter 11.) After you apply a filter or perform a selection query on a table, only the records that match the filter or query criteria remain visible. All other records are temporarily hidden from view, enabling you to concentrate on the records of interest.

About Filtering

Applying a filter is the quickest, simplest way to select a subset of records to examine. Access provides filtering commands (**Figure 10.1**) that you can issue when viewing a datasheet, form, or the results of a query, as follows:

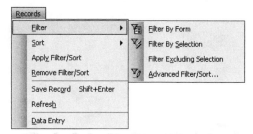

Figure 10.1 Choose filtering commands from the Records menu.

- ◆ **Filter By Selection.** Filter the current table based on the contents of the selected field.

- ◆ **Filter Excluding Selection.** Display all records that do *not* match the contents of the selected field.

- ◆ **Filter For Input.** Type an expression in a pop-up menu to specify a filtering criterion for the current field.

- ◆ **Filter By Form.** Set filtering criteria for one or multiple fields using a special form.

- ◆ **Advanced Filter/Sort.** Specify filtering criteria *and* sorting instructions for one or multiple fields using a special form.

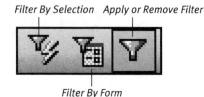

Figure 10.2 Filtering commands can also be found on the toolbar.

Here are some additional facts about filtering that you should know:

- ◆ Filtering by selection and form can be initiated by clicking a toolbar icon (**Figure 10.2**). Filtering for input can only be initiated by right-clicking in the criterion field.

- ◆ You can also filter subforms and subdatasheets.

- ◆ Filtering is cumulative; that is, you can issue additional Filter commands to further refine the displayed record subset.

- ◆ To revert to viewing all records (or the initial query results) in the default sort order, choose Records > Remove Filter/Sort or click the Remove Filter toolbar icon. After doing so, you can reapply the most recent filter by clicking the Apply Filter toolbar icon or choosing Records > Apply Filter/Sort.

Deleting a Filter

The Remove Filter/Sort command enables you to revert to the original state of a datasheet, form, or query result. However, the last filter applied to the particular object is still available and can be reapplied at any time.

To *delete* a filter (regardless of the method used to create it), open the datasheet, form, or query result; choose Records > Filter > Advanced Filter/Sort; click the Clear Grid toolbar icon (to simultaneously remove all filter criteria and sort instructions); and then click the Apply Filter toolbar icon. Essentially, this procedure replaces the previous filter with one that unfilters the datasheet, form, or query result by applying blank criteria to it.

ABOUT FILTERING

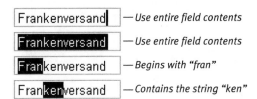

Figure 10.3 To set the filter criterion, position the cursor in the field or select all or part of a field's text.

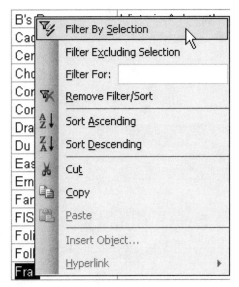

Figure 10.4 This pop-up menu appears when you right-click anywhere within the criterion field.

Filter By Selection

Of the filtering commands, this is by far the simplest to use. Rather than typing criteria, all you have to do is find a record that contains the match criterion in one of its fields.

To filter by selection:

1. In a table, form, or query result, find a field in a record that contains the criterion by which you want to filter.

    You can use the entire contents of a field as the criterion, a single word, or even as little as one character.

2. *Do one of the following* (**Figure 10.3**):

    ▲ To use the entire contents of the field as the criterion, select the entire field or simply position the cursor within the field (selecting nothing).

    ▲ To filter using the starting characters of a field as the criterion, select those characters. (Only fields that begin with those characters will be returned.)

    ▲ To filter using character(s) that appear *anywhere* within a field as the criterion, select those characters.

3. *Do one of the following:*

    ▲ Choose Records >Filter > Filter By Selection (see Figure 10.1).

    ▲ Click the Filter By Selection toolbar icon (see Figure 10.2).

    ▲ Right-click in the criterion field and choose Filter By Selection from the pop-up menu that appears (**Figure 10.4**).

    The table, form, or query is filtered to match the criterion. The remaining records (if any) are displayed.

✔ Tips

■ Select a blank field to view all records in which that field is empty.

■ You can create a subset from contiguous records in a datasheet or a query result by drag-selecting a field across several records and then issuing a Filter By Selection.

Filter Excluding Selection

This filtering command produces the opposite result of Filter By Selection. All records that do *not* match the selected criterion are displayed.

To filter by selection:

1. In a table, form, or query result, find a field in a record that contains the criterion by which you want to filter.

You can use the entire contents of a field as the criterion, a single word, or even as little as one character.

2. *Do one of the following* (see Figure 10.3):

▲ To use the entire contents of the field as the criterion, select the entire field or simply position the cursor within the field.

▲ To filter using the starting characters of a field as the criterion, select those characters. (Only fields that begin with those characters will be hidden.)

▲ To filter using character(s) that appear *anywhere* within a field as the criterion, select those characters.

3. *Do one of the following:*

▲ Choose Records >Filter > Filter Excluding Selection (see Figure 10.1).

▲ Right-click in the criterion field and choose Filter By Selection from the pop-up menu that appears (see Figure 10.4).

The table, form, or query is filtered to hide all records that match the criterion.

✔ Tip

■ To view records that have *any* entry in a given field (that is, ones in which the field isn't empty), select an instance where that field is blank. (You can use the blank record at the bottom of the datasheet.)

Filter For text box

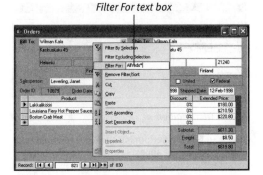

Figure 10.5 Right-click in the field on which you want to filter and enter criteria in the Filter For text box.

Filter For Input

Use this command to filter the current table by typing criteria for a single field (**Table 10.1**). You can combine criteria by using And or Or. Wildcard characters can also be used.

To filter by input:

1. In any record in a table, form, or query result, right-click the field on which you want to filter.

2. In the pop-up menu that appears, enter the filter criterion or criteria in the Filter For text box (**Figure 10.5**).

3. Press (Return) or (Enter) to execute the Filter By Input command.

✔ Tips

■ To keep the pop-up menu open in order to enter additional criteria, complete your entry by pressing (Tab) rather than (Return) or (Enter).

■ For additional help, see "About using wild-card characters" in Microsoft Access Help.

Table 10.1

Examples of Entering Filter Criteria	
EXAMPLE	FILTER RESULTS
>= 10	Records where the field's value is 10 or greater
>= 5 and <= 15	Records where the field's value is between 5 and 15, inclusive
< 5 or > 15	Records where the field's value is less than 5 or greater than 15, exclusive
> G	Records where the field's value begins with a letter that comes after G
>= 10/98	Records where the field's value is October 1, 1998 or a more recent date
Steve	Records where the field contains "Steve" (an exact match, ignoring letter case)
Steve*	Records where the field's value begins with "Steve" followed by zero or more characters; *Steve, Steven,* and *Steve Simpson* would be returned as matches, but *Jim Stevenson* would not
steve	Records where the text string "steve" is found somewhere within the field; *Steve* and *John Stevens* would both be returned as matches
b?d	Records where the field contains *bad, bed, bid,* or *bud,* but not *bead* (the ? is a wildcard for a single character); an underscore character (_) can be used in place of a question mark (?)
b[ai]d	Records where the field contains only *bad* or *bid*; it must match one of the characters in brackets
Between A and Dolan	Records where the field contains text that is alphabetically before *Dolan*
Between 10 and 20	Records where the field contains a numeric amount between 10.0 and 20.0, inclusive
Is Null	Records where the field is blank (use Is Not Null to find records where the field contains *any* data)

Filter By Form

When you opt to Filter By Form, you're presented with a blank, single-record datasheet, form, or query (depending on what you're doing when you issue the command). You can type the filtering criteria or select them from drop-down lists that match the field's contents across all records. You can filter on one or multiple fields, and wildcard characters (see Table 10.1) can be included.

To filter by form:

1. Open the form, datasheet, or query result that you want to filter.

2. Click the Filter By Form toolbar icon (see Figure 10.2) or choose Records > Filter > Filter By Form.

    If you're working with a datasheet or query, a one-line form appears (**Figure 10.6**). If you're working with a form, a blank copy of the custom form appears (**Figure 10.7**).

3. Click the first field on which you want to filter. Select a value from the field's drop-down list or type the criterion into the field.

4. *Optional:* To add an additional criterion (creating an AND filter), repeat Step 3 using a different field.

    For example, you could filter a table to show only records for a given city *and* state.

5. *Optional:* To create an OR filter (in which all matching records must meet one criterion or another), click the Or tab at the bottom of the form. A new, blank form appears. Click the field on which you want to filter, and select an existing field value from the field's drop down-list or type the criterion into the field.

6. To add other criteria, repeat Steps 3–5.

7. Choose Filter > Apply Filter/Sort or click the Apply Filter toolbar icon.

    The results are displayed in the original datasheet, form, or query.

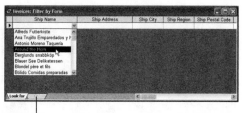

Add an OR condition

Figure 10.6 When performing a filter by form, either a one-line datasheet appears (when initiated from a datasheet or query) ...

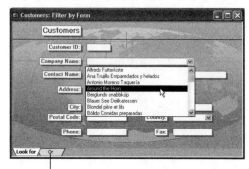

Add an OR condition

Figure 10.7 ... or a copy of the current form appears.

Queries from Filters

You can create a query from any Filter By Form or Advanced Filter/Sort. With the filter displayed, click the Save As Query toolbar icon or choose File > Save As Query. Enter a name for the query in the Save As Query dialog box and click OK. The query is added as a new Query object.

FILTER BY FORM

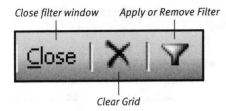

Close filter window   Apply or Remove Filter

Clear Grid

Figure 10.8 Click the Clear Grid toolbar icon to clear a previous set of filter criteria.

✔ Tips

- In a form that contains check boxes, option buttons, or toggle buttons, you can filter by their state. Click to check, select, uncheck, or unselect them, as desired.

- If you issue a second Filter By Form command—even after removing the effects of the previous Filter By Form—the original criteria are automatically selected.

- To clear all filtering criteria from the current form, click the Clear Grid toolbar icon (**Figure 10.8**) or choose Edit > Clear Grid.

- To remove an existing OR condition, click its tab at the bottom of the form and then choose Edit > Delete Tab.

- As with the other Filter commands, you can remove the effects of a Filter By Form by clicking the Remove Filter toolbar icon or choosing Records > Remove Filter/Sort.

Reusing Filters

Complex filters take time to create. As explained in the points below, you don't have to go to the trouble of re-creating a filter each time you need it.

- Every filter that you create is associated only with the object to which it is applied; namely, a particular datasheet or form.

- If you save a datasheet, form, or query after applying a filter, the filter is saved, too. The next time you open that data-sheet, form, or query, you can apply the saved filter by clicking the Apply Filter toolbar icon or by choosing Records > Apply Filter/Sort.

- If you create a filter for a subdatasheet or subform, save the changes, and later open the *actual* datasheet or form, the filter can be applied there, too.

FILTER BY FORM

Advanced Filter/Sort

The advantage of using Advanced Filter/Sort over Filter By Form is that you can create complex filters for the current datasheet, form, or query results while simultaneously specifying sort instructions. In addition, it is the only filtering method that allows you to mix ascending and descending sort orders.

To filter using Advanced Filter/Sort:

1. Open the form, datasheet, or query result that you want to filter.

2. Choose Records > Filter > Advanced Filter/Sort.

   A Filter window opens (**Figure 10.9**).

3. *Optional:* If criteria are already displayed that you don't want to use, you can clear them all by clicking the Clear Grid toolbar icon or by choosing Edit > Clear Grid.

   You can manually clear an individual criterion by deleting it or replacing it with a new criterion.

4. Each column in the Filter window can contain a filter criterion or a sort instruction. Starting from the leftmost column, select a field from the Field drop-down list (**Figure 10.10**) and then do any of the following:

   ▲ In the Criteria text box, type a filter criterion related to the selected field.

   ▲ In the Criteria text box, create a filter criterion for the selected field with the assistance of the Expression Builder (**Figure 10.11**) by right-clicking in the text box and choosing Build.

   ▲ In the Sort text box, select Ascending or Descending to sort the table on the selected field.

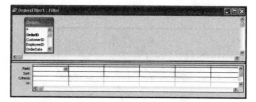

Figure 10.9 Enter filter criteria and sort instructions in the Filter window.

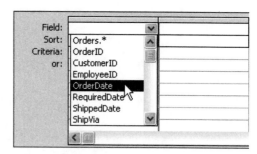

Figure 10.10 Click the right end of any Field or Sort text box to reveal a drop-down field list or sort order menu, respectively.

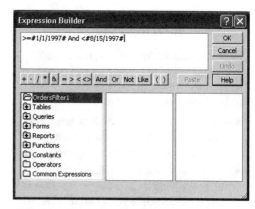

Figure 10.11 You can use the Expression Builder to help create a complicated filter criterion.

5. *Optional:* To add an OR condition for the selected field, type it in the Or text box or create it using the Expression Builder.

   When the column is used to specify an OR condition, the filter criteria will be satisfied by any record that fulfills the original criterion *or* the OR condition.

6. To add other filter criteria or additional sort instructions, move to the next column and repeat Steps 4 and 5.

7. To execute the filter and sort instructions, click the Apply Filter toolbar icon (see Figure 10.8) or choose Filter > Apply Filter/Sort.

   The Filter window closes and the form, datasheet, or query results window reappears, filtered and sorted per your instructions.

✔ Tips

- You can specify an AND condition as a criterion for a single field. To satisfy the criterion, both parts must be true. For example, to find records within a range of dates, you might enter:

  >= 1/1/97 And <= 8/15/97

- To create an AND filter for multiple fields, specify multiple criteria across the columns in the Filter window. For example, to find sales records in the second quarter of 2003, you would select Year as the first column's field and enter *2003* as the criterion. Then select Quarter as the second column's field and enter *2* as the criterion.

- Sorts in the Filter window are performed from left to right. Specify the most important sort fields first and then proceed to the less important ones; that is, the "tie breakers." To learn more about sorting, see Chapter 9.

ADVANCED FILTER/SORT

WORKING WITH QUERIES

Queries are built from fields in your tables or in other existing queries that enable you to ask questions about the contents of a database. You can use queries to find records within one table or to combine the contents of several related tables into a single, easy-to-read object.

You can do more than simple record-finding with queries. A query can include calculations like sums, averages, and even standard deviations. These calculations can make your results more meaningful and easier to interpret.

The results of a query are called a *dynaset*, short for "dynamic set" of records. The collection is dynamic because it changes when the query changes, such as when you pull data from different fields or perform new calculations on the results. These changes, however radical, don't affect the data in the source tables or queries.

In this chapter, you'll learn the essentials of creating queries, including the following:

◆ Creating queries using wizards and modifying them in Design View

◆ Specifying query criteria manually and with the assistance of the Expression Builder

◆ Using wildcards in criteria expressions

◆ Working with SQL

◆ Creating a crosstab query

The Query Design Window

When you design a query, you need to specify which tables and queries you want to use as data sources, select fields from those tables and queries that contain the information you want, and set criteria so that the desired records are found. You make these choices in the query design grid (**Figure 11.1**).

◆ **Menu bar.** The menu bar presents all normal and query-related commands.

◆ **Query Design toolbar.** This toolbar provides many of the basic commands you'll use when working with queries.

◆ **Table area.** This area shows the tables you have chosen to work with in your query.

◆ **Query design grid.** This is where you create your query. You specify the name of a field, the table in which it appears, whether you want to sort on the field, whether the field should be shown in the query results, and what criteria you want to use to select records based on a field's content. The configuration of the query design grid changes depending on the type of query you're constructing. **Figure 11.1** shows the query design grid for a select query.

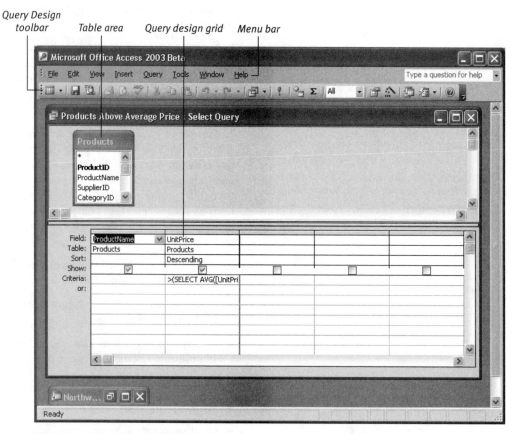

Figure 11.1 A select query in Design View.

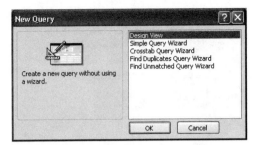

Figure 11.2 Select a query wizard from the New Query dialog box.

Select a table or query

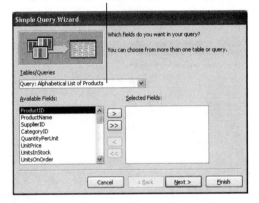

Figure 11.3 Select a table or query on which to base the new query, and move the fields you wish to include into the Selected Fields list.

Creating Queries with a Wizard

You can quickly create queries using Access wizards. The most basic query is a select query in which records are selected from tables or other queries. See the sidebar later in this chapter to learn about the many types of queries you can create with the query wizards.

You can use the Simple Query Wizard to create two variants of a select query: a *detail query* (which shows every field in the query results) and a *summary query* (which summarizes by presenting the sum, average, maximum, or minimum for select numerical fields).

To create a query with a wizard:

1. Select Queries in the Objects pane of the Database window and click the New toolbar icon.

   The New Query dialog box appears (**Figure 11.2**). A brief description of the currently selected query type appears in the left side of the dialog box.

2. Select Simple Query Wizard and click OK.

   The first screen of the wizard appears (**Figure 11.3**).

3. From the Tables/Queries drop-down list, select an existing table or query from which you want to draw fields.

4. Add fields to the Selected Fields list by clicking the > (add a field) or >> (add all fields) buttons. To remove fields, click the < (remove a field) or << (remove all fields) buttons.

   If desired, you can include related fields from other tables and queries. Repeat Steps 3 and 4, as necessary. Click Next.

   continues on next page

5. Indicate whether you want to create a detail or summary query (**Figure 11.4**). A *detail query* shows record data for every specified field. A *summary query* presents summary statistics for selected numerical fields.

6. If you've selected Summary, click the Summary Options button. Click check boxes on the Summary Options screen (**Figure 11.5**) to select statistics to calculate for each field. To display a record count as one of the query columns, click the bottom check box. Click OK to return to the previous screen.

7. Click Next to display the final wizard screen.

8. Enter a name for the query and click Finish.

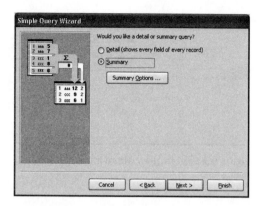

Figure 11.4 You can display every value or have Access summarize the contents of selected fields.

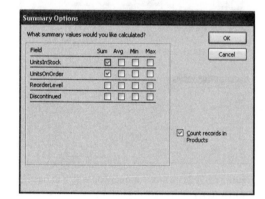

Figure 11.5 Choose the fields you want Access to summarize and the summary method(s) for each.

Types of Queries

Access lets you go far beyond elementary select queries; you won't even need to jump through hoops to create the different query types. Here's a quick rundown of the types that are available to you:

◆ **Select query.** The basic query type; a select query finds and displays selected data fields.

◆ **Parameter query.** Like select queries, but you're prompted for the criteria (*parameters*) to use when selecting data.

◆ **Crosstab query.** Crosstab queries generate spreadsheet-like output based on data from three or more fields. A standard query's results relate a series of fields (such as Title, Publisher, ISBN) to a single thing (such as a book). A crosstab query relates a single field (such as Sales) to two things (such as Publisher and Book).

◆ **Delete query.** Finds records and then deletes them. Make sure that's what you want to do!

◆ **Update query.** Finds records and changes one or more of their values, such as increasing the prices of items from a particular supplier.

◆ **Append query.** Takes records from one or more tables and adds them to the end of other tables.

◆ **Make-table query.** Selects a set of records and creates a table from them (rather than a dynaset).

◆ **Find duplicates query.** Looks for records in a table that have the same value in one or more fields.

◆ **Find unmatched query.** Looks for records in one table that have no corresponding records in another table, such as a customer with no orders.

Viewing Queries in Design View

Working with queries is fairly easy, but it may take some time to get them working exactly the way you want. And if you change the structure of the tables you're querying (by deleting a field or moving it from one table to another, for example), you may need to modify your queries to reflect the changes. Modifications to queries are done in Design View.

To view or alter a query in Design View:

1. Display all existing queries for your database by clicking the Queries icon in the Objects pane of the Database window.

2. Select the query that you want to view and click the Design toolbar icon.

   The query appears in the query design grid, along with the tables used to generate the results (see Figure 11.1).

✔ Tips

- The type of icon that precedes a query name in the Database window reflects the type of query it is.

- If you need to modify a query while viewing its results in Datasheet View, you can switch to Design View by choosing View > Design View or by clicking the View toolbar icon.

- Remember to periodically save your work by choosing File > Save or by clicking the Save toolbar icon.

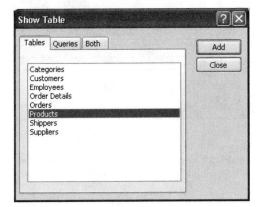

Figure 11.6 Click the Show Table toolbar icon.

Figure 11.7 Select additional tables or queries from which you'd like to draw fields.

Choosing Tables to Query

When creating or modifying a query in Design View, you can select the tables from which you want to draw fields—adding or removing tables as needed. If you think you might need a field from a particular table but aren't sure, you can include the table anyway. You can always remove it later.

For example, suppose that you want to create a query to find all books by a certain author. You think you may also want to display the author's contact information in the query results. In addition to the Books table (containing information about titles), you can add the Authors table (containing author contact information) to your query. If you later decide that you don't want to display the contact information in the query results, you can hide the Authors table.

To add a table to a query:

1. Open the query in Design View.

   Select the query name in the Database window and click the Design toolbar icon, or create a new query in Design View.

2. Click the Show Table toolbar icon (**Figure 11.6**), choose Query > Show Table, or right-click a blank spot in the query design window and choose Show Table from the pop-up menu.

   The Show Table dialog box appears, listing all the tables and queries in the database (**Figure 11.7**).

3. Select the name of the table or query that you want to make available to the current query. Click Add.

4. When you're done adding tables, click Close.

✔ Tip

■ To remove a table from the query design window, right-click the table's title bar and choose Remove Table from the pop-up menu that appears.

Adding Fields to a Query

In Design View, you can add fields to a query from any table or query that is *shown* in (added to) the query design window, as explained in the previous section. The purpose of adding a field is to accomplish at least one of the following:

◆ You want to sort on the field.

◆ You want to include the field as part of the query's record selection/search criteria.

◆ You want the field to be displayed in the query results.

To choose fields to include in a query:

1. Open or create a query in Design View, show the tables and queries from which you want to draw fields, and click the title bar of the table containing the first field that you want to add.

2. Select the desired field and drag it to the first open Field cell in the grid at the bottom of the window (**Figure 11.8**).

3. *Do any (or all) of the following:*

   ▲ To designate the field as a sort field, choose Ascending or Descending from the drop-down list in the Sort cell.

   ▲ To base all or part of the record selection/search criteria on an expression related to the field, enter the expression in the Criteria cell (as explained in the following sections).

   ▲ To display the field in the query results, ensure that Show is checked.

✔ Tips

■ To add all of the fields from a table to the query, drag the table's asterisk (*) designator into an empty Field cell in the grid.

■ You can also add fields by clicking in an open Field cell, opening its drop-down menu, and selecting the field name (**Figure 11.9**).

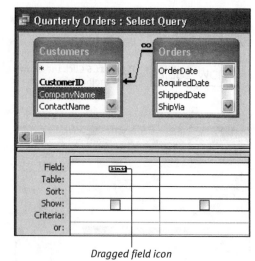

Dragged field icon

Figure 11.8 Select a field name from the active table and drag it into the first open Field cell.

Click to open the field list

Figure 11.9 You can also add a field by selecting its name from the Field drop-down list. Note that the table name precedes each field name.

Specifying Query Criteria

You're almost done. You've chosen the tables you want and selected the necessary fields from them. All that's left is to tell Access which records to pull from your tables. You do this by entering *criteria* at the bottom of each field column that you want to use to select records.

If you're looking for a specific value in a field, simply type that value in the field's Criteria cell. If you're working with bibliographic information data, you could type **1996** or =**1996** in the Criteria cell of the Copyright Year field to find all books published in 1996. You can also use *operators* in criteria, such as > (greater than), < (less than), and <> (not equal to). For example, to identify sales that were larger than $10,000, you'd enter >**10000**.

Using text strings as criteria is also easy, but you do need to enclose them in quotes. To find all of the books published by Peachpit Press, you would type **"Peachpit Press"** in the Criteria cell. The <, >, and <> operators can be used with text strings as well. For example, >**"Peachpit"** would return any books by a publisher with a name that alphabetically follows Peachpit.

Date comparisons are similar, but you need to indicate that the criterion value is a date by typing it in the M/D/Y format and surrounding the date with pound signs. For example, August 2, 1968 would be written as **#8/2/68#**. See **Tables 11.1–11.5** for a list of other operators that you can use in query criteria.

✔ Tip

■ If you have trouble remembering how to enter specific kinds of criteria, Access will do its best to reformat what you type or paste into any Criteria field. If you enter a text string such as **Steve**, for example, Access will change it to "Steve" for you.

Showing and Hiding Fields

Not every field specified in the query design window is worth displaying as a column in the query results datasheet. In fact, cluttering the results with irrelevant fields often makes it more difficult to concentrate on the *important* data. For example, you might want to select only the records in which a customer's State field contains "CA." There's little point in displaying the State column in the results, since—by definition—every instance will read *CA*.

To prevent a column from appearing in the results datasheet, make sure that the field's Show check box is not checked (see Figure 11.8).

Table 11.1

OPERATOR	DESCRIPTION	EXAMPLE	NOTES
*	Multiplication	4*3 = 12	
+	Addition	4+3 = 7	
-	Subtraction	4-3 = 1	
/	Division	4/3 = 1.333…	
\	Integer division	4\3 = 1	The result is truncated, not rounded.
^	Exponentiation	4^3 = 64	
Mod	Modulo (remainder) division	7 Mod 3 = 1	7/3 = 2 with a remainder of 1, so 7 Mod 3 = 1

Table 11.2

Relational Operators

OPERATOR	DESCRIPTION	EXAMPLE
=	Equal	Pages = 100
<>	Not Equal	Pages <> 101
<	Less Than	Pages < 200
>	Greater Than	Pages > 50
<=	Less Than or Equal to	Pages <= 1000
>=	Greater Than or Equal to	Pages >= 100

Table 11.3

String Operators

OPERATOR	DESCRIPTION	EXAMPLE
&	Concatenation	("Eric" & " and " & "Deb") returns "Eric and Deb"
Like	Similar to	Like "comm" returns "community," "commonality," and "telecommunications"

Table 11.4

Logical (Boolean) Operators

OPERATOR	DESCRIPTION	EXAMPLE	NOTES
And	Logical And	A And B	Both A and B are true.
Or	Logical Or	A Or B	Either A or B (or both) is true.
Xor	Exclusive Or	A Xor B	Either A or B (but not both) is true.
Not	Negates the affected expression	Not (A Or B)	Neither A nor B is true.

Table 11.5

Miscellaneous Operators

OPERATOR	DESCRIPTION	EXAMPLE
Between…and	Between two values (inclusive)	Books.Publisher Between "Peachpit" and "Wiley"
In (list)	The value occurs in an enumerated list	In ("Peachpit", "O'Reilly", "Wiley")
Is Null	The field or calculation returns a null value (not zero)	Is Null (Books.ISBN)

SPECIFYING QUERY CRITERIA

Using Wildcards in Criteria

Wildcards are characters that represent one or more characters in an expression. For instance, to find names that begin with "B," you can set the criterion to **"B*"**. The asterisk wildcard tells Access to find every record where the value in the Last Name field begins with the letter "B" and is followed by zero or more additional characters.

The three wildcard characters you'll use most are the asterisk (*), which matches any number of characters (**"Bl*"** returns Blank, Block, and Bly); the question mark (?), which matches any single character (**"Bl?ck"** returns Black and Block, but not Blosovick); and the pound sign (#), which returns any single digit (**"199#"** returns 1999 and 1998, but not 199074).

✔ Tips

■ If you want to search for wildcard characters in your records, surround the character in square brackets ([]). For example, if you want to find records containing an asterisk, your criteria would be **"[*]"**.

■ An underscore (_) character can be used instead of the question mark (?) wildcard, and a percentage (%) symbol can be substituted for an asterisk (*) wildcard.

The Expression Builder

It can be difficult to remember table and field names. If you must also remember the comparison and arithmetic operators that you can use in criteria, the challenge can become monumental. Rather than requiring you to type criteria directly into the query grid, Access provides a handy tool called the Expression Builder that you can use to create criteria and other expressions. The Expression Builder provides a larger working area than a Criteria cell, contains a list of every table and field in your database, and provides a complete list of the operators that you can use. The more common operators are presented as buttons.

In Access, an *expression* is a series of field names, operators, and values used to find records or calculate values. For example, the criteria "[Sales.Subtotal] > 1500" is an expression, as is "[Sales.Subtotal] * .07".

To use the Expression Builder:

1. Open a query in Design View.

2. Click the Criteria cell in which you want the criteria to appear, and click the Build toolbar icon (**Figure 11.10**). Or you can right-click the Criteria cell and choose Build from the pop-up menu.

    The Expression Builder appears.

3. To create the expression (**Figure 11.11**), you ean combine any of these actions:

    ▲ Type text, numbers, and other values.

    ▲ Click an operator button in the center of the screen.

    ▲ Expand folders in the first list box to view your tables and fields, operators, built-in functions, and so on. To enter one of these items into the expression, double-click the item or select the item and click Paste.

    Click OK when you're done. The expression appears in the Criteria cell.

Figure 11.10 To open the Expression Builder, click the Build toolbar icon.

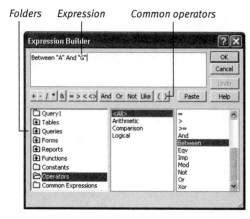

Figure 11.11 You can create or examine expressions in the Expression Builder.

THE EXPRESSION BUILDER

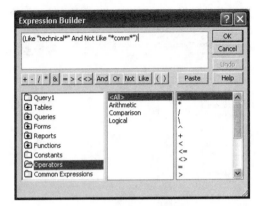

Figure 11.12 Type, click buttons, and/or select components to create the first part of the expression.

Creating Advanced Criteria

Although the Expression Builder is relatively easy to use, it can take a little time to fully understand how it works. In the following pages, you'll learn how to use the Expression Builder to create more complex criteria.

In this example, we'll construct a criterion that returns titles in a Library table that begin with the word "technical," but do *not* contain the fragment "comm"—unless it co-occurs with the word "international." In other words, we want the query to find the book entitled *Technical Communities International*, but not one named *Technical Communicating*.

To create an advanced criteria with the Expression Builder:

1. Create or open a query in Design View. Click the Criteria cell of the column representing the field for which you want to set criteria.

   For this example, the field is named Title.

2. Open the Expression Builder.

3. Create the first part of the expression (**Figure 11.12**):

   (Like "technical*" And Not Like "*comm*")

   Let's break this down. Like "technical*" tells Access to look for titles that begin with the word "technical." The trailing asterisk tells Access that other characters (or words) can optionally follow "technical." The second half of the fragment—And Not Like "*comm*"—uses the And and Not operators to add a second condition to the expression. It tells Access to ignore books with words like "communication" and "communicating" anywhere in the title.

   If we stopped at this point, we'd find every title that began with the word "technical," but did not contain words like "communications."

continues on next page

CREATING ADVANCED CRITERIA

4. Now we can add the second part of the expression:

(Like "technical*" And Like "*comm*" And Like "*international*")

In this part of the criteria, we will find all titles that begin with "technical," contain text such as "communication" or "communicating," and also contain the word "international." The latter two text strings can occur anywhere in the title, as long as they follow "technical" (the first word). Because we want all three text strings to occur in the title, we use the And operator to separate them.

5. Now that we have both key parts of the expression, we need to link them so that Access returns titles that meet *either* half of the expression.

To accomplish this, you use the Or operator. Using And would require the title to meet both halves of the criteria, and thus return no values. Why? Because the first half looks for titles in which "technical*" and "*comm*" do *not* occur together, while the second half looks for titles in which they *do* occur together.

The complete criteria expression (**Figure 11.13**) looks like this:

(Like "technical*" And Not Like "*comm*") Or (Like "technical*" And Like "*comm*" And Like "*international*")

6. Click OK to close the Expression Builder.

7. Click the Run toolbar icon (**Figure 11.14**) or choose Query > Run to execute the query and view the results (**Figure 11.15**).

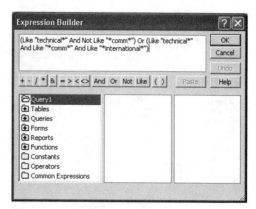

Figure 11.13 The complete criteria looks like this.

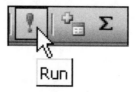

Figure 11.14 To execute the query, click the Run toolbar icon.

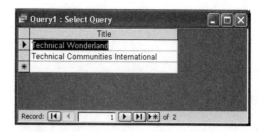

Figure 11.15 The query returns two titles beginning with the word "Technical"—one without the "comm" string and a second with both the "comm" and the "international" text strings.

Introducing SQL

SQL (Structured Query Language) is a standardized way of forming databases and writing queries to extract information from those databases. You'll encounter SQL if you ever work with Access Projects, which let you create an Access-like interface for a database on an SQL server.

The following is an example of an SQL query:

SELECT DISTINCTROW Topics.Topic, Books.Title, Books.URL

FROM Topics INNER JOIN (Books INNER JOIN BookTopics ON Books.BookID = BookTopics.BookID) ON Topics.TopicID = BookTopics.TopicID;

The first element of the statement is the SELECT command. It tells Access which fields you want to pull from the tables. In this case, we want to retrieve values from the Topics table's Topic field, and the Title and URL fields from the Books table. The DISTINCTROW command tells the database to insert a carriage return after each set of values returned by the query.

FROM Topics INNER JOIN (Books INNER JOIN BookTopics ON Books.BookID = BookTopics.BookID)

This element identifies which records to examine. The FROM statement combines records from the Books and BookTopics tables, where the records have the same value in the BookID field.

ON Topics.TopicID = BookTopics.TopicID;

After Access obtains those records, it combines them with records from the Topics table where the value in the two tables' TopicsID fields match. The semicolon at the end of the statement indicates that no additional commands follow.

Querying with SQL

SQL is a flexible, powerful language that lets you specify precisely which records and fields you want to use in a query. In fact, you're working in SQL whenever you create an Access query. Access automatically translates your queries to SQL. To see the SQL source behind a query, simply open the query and choose View > SQL View.

SQL View shows the actions that Access takes when it creates and runs the query. Because SQL is common to many database applications, creating queries in Access and then examining their SQL equivalents can help you understand how SQL queries are created to interact with non-Access databases.

To create an SQL query:

1. In Design View, create a query or open an existing one.

2. Choose View > SQL View.

   A window appears, containing the SQL equivalent of the current query (**Figure 11.16**). The text is already selected for copying.

3. Copy the text in the window by pressing Ctrl C or by choosing Edit > Copy.

4. Click wherever you want to insert the SQL statement (in a Visual Basic code module or a Properties box, for example), and press Ctrl V or choose Edit > Paste to paste it.

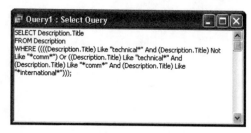

Figure 11.16 This lengthy SQL statement was generated from the advanced query example presented earlier in the chapter.

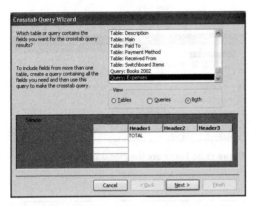

Figure 11.17 Select a table or query on which to base the crosstab query.

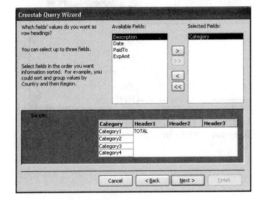

Figure 11.18 Select the row field(s) for the query.

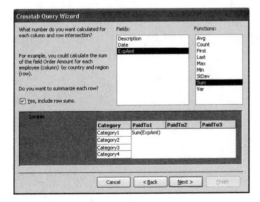

Figure 11.19 Select the data value field and a summary function that you want to calculate for it.

Creating a Crosstab Query

Crosstab queries are like spreadsheets in that they both summarize data based on three values: a row value, a column value, and data that represents the intersection of a row and column. In the following example, you'll see how you can use a crosstab query to present expense amounts (the data), broken down by expense category (row values) and payee (column values).

To create a crosstab query:

1. Select Queries in the Objects pane of the Database window, and click the New toolbar icon.

   The New Query dialog box appears.

2. Select Crosstab Query Wizard and click OK.

   The Crosstab Query Wizard appears (**Figure 11.17**).

3. Click a View radio button to indicate whether tables, queries, or both from the current database should be listed. Select a single table or query from which to draw fields for the crosstab query. Click Next.

4. Move one or more fields that will serve as row headings into the Selected Fields list (**Figure 11.18**). Click Next.

   The Sample area shows how the selected field(s) will be arranged on the datasheet.

5. Do the same for the field or fields that will serve as column headings. Click Next.

6. Select the data value field and the function (such as Sum or Min) that will be calculated for the field (**Figure 11.19**). To also display row sums, be sure that the check box for "Yes, include row sums" is checked. Click Next.

7. In the final screen, name the query and click Finish.

   The crosstab query appears in a new window (**Figure 11.20**).

✔ Tips

- The Crosstab Query Wizard limits you to working with values found in one table or query. If you want to use this wizard, you'll have to prepare a table or query that has the necessary fields beforehand.

- You can also create a crosstab query entirely in Design View:

  - ▲ Begin by creating a select query on which to base the crosstab query.

  - ▲ Choose Query > Crosstab Query. A Crosstab row is added to the query design grid.

  - ▲ Select Row Heading from the Crosstab drop-down list in one field and Column Heading from another field.

  - ▲ Click the Crosstab cell in the column that will serve as the data values. Choose Values from the drop-down list.

  - ▲ Click in the Total cell of the same column and choose a summary statistic, such as Sum or Avg (**Figure 11.21**).

  - ▲ Click the Run toolbar icon to execute the query.

Sum of the ExpAmt field

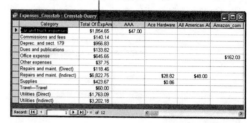

Figure 11.20 These are the crosstab query results.

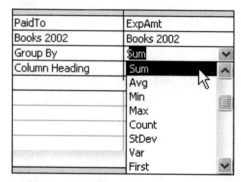

Figure 11.21 In the data value's column, select a summary statistic from the Total cell's drop-down list.

12

PRINTING RECORDS

When you think of printing in Access, it's likely that you immediately think of *reports*—elaborately (or, at least, neatly) formatted data, computations, and summary calculations.

But sometimes your needs aren't so elaborate. For example, you might want to print out a small set of employee information forms. Or perhaps a sorted datasheet is all you need.

In this chapter, you'll learn the procedures for printing datasheets, forms, and query results. More elaborate printing procedures—including automating the print process—are discussed in Chapter 14, "Creating Reports."

Printing a Datasheet

When printing a datasheet, you have two options:

- ◆ Print a complete unaltered datasheet, using the current print settings.

- ◆ Print a modified datasheet by first sorting it, selecting or hiding fields, and/or selecting specific records.

To print an entire datasheet (bypassing the Print dialog box):

- ◆ *Do one of the following:*
  - ▲ In the Database window, select the table that you want to print and then click the Print toolbar icon.
  - ▲ In the Database window, right-click the table that you want to print and choose Print from the pop-up menu that appears (**Figure 12.1**).

The complete datasheet prints, using the current print settings.

To print an entire or partial datasheet (using the Print dialog box):

1. In the Database window, select or open the table that you want to print.

2. *Do any of the following:*
   - ▲ Sort the datasheet by one or more fields.
   - ▲ Hide unnecessary columns (by selecting them and choosing Format > Hide Columns or by dragging from the right edge to the left edge of the column title).
   - ▲ Select a contiguous group of records to print by drag-selecting or [Shift]-clicking their record indicators.
   - ▲ Filter the records to show only a subset.
   - ▲ Select a rectangular range of data to print (**Figure 12.2**).

3. Choose File > Print or press [Ctrl] [P]. The Print dialog box appears (**Figure 12.3**).

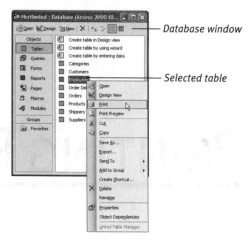

Database window

Selected table

Figure 12.1 You can print a table by right-clicking it and choosing Print from the pop-up menu.

Figure 12.2 You can print selected records or—as shown here—a selected data range.

Destination printer   *Printer settings*

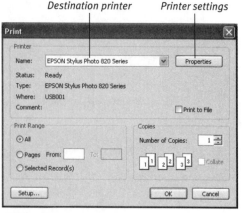

Figure 12.3 Select a printer and set print options in the Print dialog box.

Figure 12.4 Set printer-specific options in the Properties dialog box.

Figure 12.5 Change the margins on this tab of the Page Setup dialog box.

Figure 12.6 Set the paper size, orientation, and feed method on this tab.

4. Select the destination printer from the Name drop-down list.

5. *Optional:* Click the Properties button to set options for the current print job, such as black-and-white or color printing and the paper orientation (**Figure 12.4**). Click OK after viewing or changing the settings.

Options in the printer's Properties dialog box are specific to the selected printer.

6. *Do one of the following:*

▲ To print the entire datasheet, set the Print Range to All.

▲ To restrict the printout to a specific range of pages, set Print Range to Pages, and enter page numbers in the From and To text boxes.

▲ To print only the preselected records or data range, set the Print Range to Selected Record(s).

7. *Optional:* To print multiple copies, enter a number in the Number of Copies text box. You can instruct Access to *collate* the copies (printing one complete copy at a time) by clicking the Collate check box.

8. Click OK to begin the print job.

✔ Tips

■ Use these procedures for printing queries, too.

■ You can also change printer settings in the Page Setup dialog box (**Figures 12.5 and 12.6**). Choose File > Page Setup immediately before issuing the Print command.

■ Another way to reach the Page Setup dialog box is by clicking the Setup button at the bottom of the Print dialog box.

■ Contrary to the information in Help, you *can't* include subdatasheets as part of a datasheet printout. If you need to do this, use the Report Wizard to create a grouped report containing multiple tables (as explained in Chapter 14).

PRINTING A DATASHEET

Printing Forms

While forms are generally designed with data entry in mind, it can sometimes be useful to print them. Having a formatted printout of a person's contact information from a form can be preferable to printing it from the datasheet, for example. In addition, unlike the case with datasheets and subdatasheets, subform data *is* included in form printouts.

To print all forms in a table (bypassing the Print dialog box):

◆ *Do one of the following:*

▲ In the Database window, select the form that you want to print and then click the Print toolbar icon.

▲ In the Database window, right-click the form that you want to print and choose Print from the pop-up menu that appears (see Figure 12.1).

The complete set of forms prints (**Figure 12.7**), using the current print settings.

To print all or selected forms in a table (using the Print dialog box):

1. In the Database window, select or open the form that you want to print.

2. *Do any of the following:*

▲ Sort the table by one or more fields.

▲ Filter the records to show only a subset.

3. Choose File > Print or press Ctrl P.
The Print dialog box appears (see Figure 12.3).

4. Select the destination printer from the Name drop-down list.

5. *Optional:* Click the Properties button to set options for the current print job, such as black-and-white or color printing and the paper orientation (see Figure 12.4). Click OK after viewing or changing the settings.

Subform

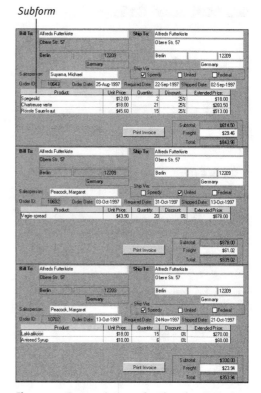

Figure 12.7 Forms print one after the other. Embedded subforms automatically expand.

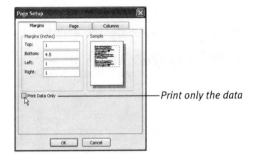

Figure 12.8 You can elect to print only form data.

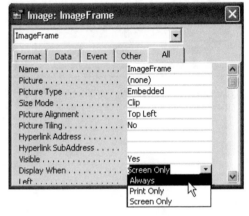

Figure 12.9 If an image on the form doesn't print, switch to Design View and change the Display When property for the field to Always or Print Only.

■ If a form has multiple sections (such as the tabbed Employee form in the Northwind sample database), only the visible section prints. To print other sections, make each one visible and reissue the Print command.

6. *Do one of the following:*

  ▲ Set the Print Range to All. (If you've filtered the data, only the remaining records will print. Otherwise, the entire table will be printed.)

  ▲ To print only the currently displayed record, set the Print Range to Selected Record(s).

7. *Optional:* To print multiple copies, enter a number in the Number of Copies text box. You can instruct Access to *collate* the copies (printing one complete copy at a time) by clicking the Collate check box.

8. Click OK to begin the print job.

✔ Tips

■ A major drawback when printing forms is that they automatically print one after another, squeezing as many onto each page as possible. A page break may come in the middle of a record. For this reason, it's often preferable to create a report instead of printing the actual forms.

■ Although you can't set page breaks when printing forms, you can adjust the margins in the Print dialog box. Set them so that exactly one form will fit on each page.

■ When printing forms, an option in the Page Setup dialog box allow you to print only the data (**Figure 12.8**), ignoring any background design. This can be useful if you've created a background from a scanned form (an insurance claim form, for example). Using this option, you can print the data onto the actual forms.

■ Images added as data to forms may not print as you expect. When printing the Employees forms in the Northwind sample database, for example, the first employee picture (in the current sort order) prints for every record. In addition, an image *only* prints if its Display When property is set to Always or Print Only (**Figure 12.9**).

PRINTING FORMS

Using Print Preview

As you undoubtedly gathered from the preceding pages in this chapter, printing forms and datasheets is fraught with *gotchas*. It's easy to print an entire 1,000-record database when all you meant to print was a handful of records, for example. To avoid wasted paper, to assure yourself that the right data will print, and to ensure that the data is formatted as you want, it's prudent to use the Print Preview command before most print jobs. Print Preview shows onscreen exactly what will be printed.

When picking a preview procedure from the step lists below, use the one that matches what you would do if you were printing.

To preview all datasheet, form, or query records:

◆ *Do one of the following:*

▲ In the Database window, select the table, form, or query to preview, and then choose File > Print Preview or click the Print Preview toolbar icon.

▲ In the Database window, right-click the table, form, or query to preview, and choose Print Preview from the pop-up menu that appears (see Figure 12.1).

The complete data set is displayed in a preview window (**Figure 12.10**). The Print Preview toolbar appears (**Table 12.1**), enabling you to perform common activities in the preview window.

Print Preview toolbar

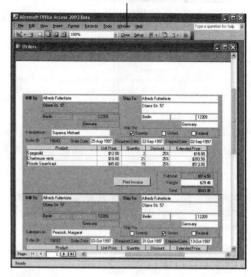

Figure 12.10 This is the first page of a set of forms displayed in print preview mode.

Table 12.1

Print Preview Toolbar Icons	
ICON	PURPOSE
🖨	Print the displayed preview data (the Print dialog box will not appear)
🔍	Toggle the zoom between displaying at actual size (100%) and the current window size (Fit)
▤ ▥ ▦	Display 1, 2, or multiple pages onscreen at the same time
Fit ▾	Select a specific zoom percentage from this drop-down list
Close	Close the print preview window and resume working with the database
Setup	Open the Page Setup dialog box to adjust margins or paper settings

To preview all or selected records in a datasheet, form, or query:

1. In the Database window, open the table, form, or query that you want to preview.

2. *Do any of the following:*

   ▲ Sort by one or more fields.

   ▲ Hide unnecessary datasheet or query columns (by selecting them and choosing Format > Hide Columns, or by dragging from the right edge to the left edge of the column title).

   ▲ Filter the records to show only a subset.

3. Choose File > Print Preview or click the Print Preview toolbar icon.

   The data is displayed in a preview window (see Figure 12.10). The Print Preview toolbar appears (see Table 12.1), enabling you to perform common activities in the preview window.

✔ Tip

■ You cannot manually select records to display in a print preview. Access automatically uses all visible records. Thus, if you need to display only particular records, selected fields, or records that match some important criteria, you should either filter the data or construct a query before issuing the Print Preview command.

USING PRINT PREVIEW

CHARTS AND PIVOTTABLES

13

The ability to create charts and graphs is something of a rarity among database applications, but certainly a *welcome* rarity. Using Microsoft Graph (an integrated component of Microsoft Office), you can add a chart to any form or report. In addition, Access has two other features (PivotTables and PivotCharts) with which you can perform rudimentary data analyses to get a better understanding of your data. Both are extremely useful when working with large, complex datasets.

In this chapter, you'll learn to create, work with, modify, and format charts, PivotTables, and PivotCharts.

About Charts

Properly constructed charts and graphs can help you summarize your data, as well as point out important trends. Surprisingly, few database applications offer charting capabilities. Access, however, can take full advantage of Microsoft Graph (the chart-making component of Office) to help you create and format charts.

A chart can be added to a form or report, and can be based on the information in any data table or query. A chart can summarize all visible data or be record-specific, changing on a record-by-record basis.

✔ Tip

- ■ Microsoft Graph isn't installed as part of the normal Office installation. The first time you try to insert a chart into a database, Office will offer to install Graph.

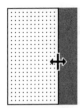

Figure 13.1 This cursor appears when you're over a grid edge you can drag.

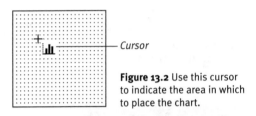

Cursor

Figure 13.2 Use this cursor to indicate the area in which to place the chart.

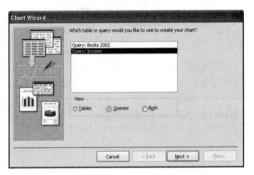

Figure 13.3 Select a table or query from which to draw the chart's data.

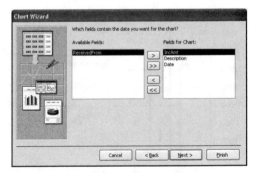

Figure 13.4 Specify the fields to use in the chart. (The order of the fields isn't important.)

Creating a Chart

The simplest way to create a chart is to use the Chart Wizard. After generating a chart, you can make any necessary changes.

To insert a chart:

1. *Do one of the following:*

   ▲ Create a new report or form (in Design View) in which to insert the chart.

   ▲ Open an existing report or form (in Design View) in which to insert the chart.

2. If necessary, enlarge the report or form so there will be room in which to place the chart.

   To expand the page horizontally, drag the right edge of the grid (**Figure 13.1**). To expand the page vertically, drag the top edge of the Page Footer.

3. Choose Insert > Chart.

   The cursor changes to a crosshair connected to a tiny chart (**Figure 13.2**).

4. Click to set the upper-left corner of the chart, or click and drag a rectangular area to set specific dimensions.

   When you release the mouse button, the Chart Wizard appears (**Figure 13.3**).

5. Select a table or query on which to base the chart, and then click Next.

   By clicking a radio button, you can restrict the list to show only tables, only queries, or both. (Basing a chart on a query enables you to restrict the data to only those records that match certain criteria.)

6. In the next screen (**Figure 13.4**), select fields on which to base the chart. Click Next.

   Click the > button to move a selected field from the Available Fields list to the Fields for Chart list; click the >> button to simultaneously move all fields.

   continues on next page

7. In the next screen, click an icon to select a chart type. Click Next.

   A description of the selected chart is presented in the right side of the window.

8. In the next screen (**Figure 13.5**), Access guesses how the selected fields should be used to create the chart. You can do any of the following:

   ▲ To change fields, drag them from the list on the right into the proper placeholder on the graph.

   ▲ To change the method used to summarize or group a field, double-click the field's placeholder (**Figure 13.6**).

   ▲ Click the Preview Chart button to see a representation of the chart as currently configured.

   Click Next to continue.

9. In the final screen, enter a title for the chart and indicate whether it should have a legend. Click Finish.

   A dummy chart with sample data appears on the form or report page.

10. If the chart isn't proportional, drag a corner until it displays properly. To view the actual chart (**Figure 13.7**), choose View > Form View (for a form) or View > Print Preview (for a report).

✔ Tips

■ Each placeholder is meant for a specific type of data. In a bar chart, for example, the Y axis (upper-left) generally contains numeric data, and the X axis (bottom) contains a categorical value, such as Males and Females or months of the year. A bar chart can optionally include a series (right) by which to break the data into groups.

■ After you save the form or report, the chart will always show actual rather than sample data. You'll find it easier to edit a chart after it's been saved.

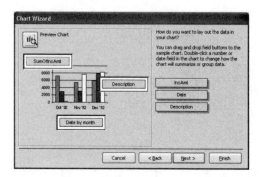

Figure 13.5 Specify fields to use by dragging them into the chart placeholders.

Figure 13.6 You can double-click a grouping or summary placeholder to change its settings.

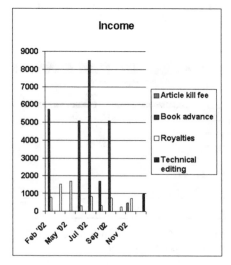

Figure 13.7 A finished chart in preview mode.

Selected chart   Datasheet

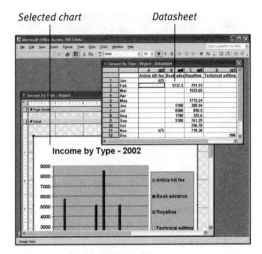

Income by Type - 2002

Figure 13.8 When a chart is double-clicked, its datasheet automatically appears.

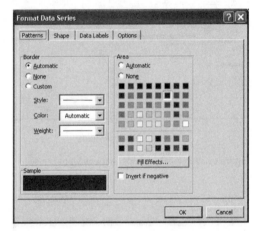

Figure 13.9 Double-click a chart element to bring up an appropriate dialog box in which you can change the element's properties.

Figure 13.10 A ScreenTip shows the element that's selected.

Modifying a Chart

The Chart Wizard will present you with a reasonably formatted chart. However, you can often make it more attractive by making some simple modifications.

To modify a chart:

1. In the Database window, double-click the form or report that contains the chart.

2. Change to Design View (click the View toolbar icon or choose View > Design View).

3. Double-click the chart to select it for editing in Microsoft Graph (**Figure 13.8**).

4. Select the part of the chart that you want to modify, such as the legend box, a legend color block, a data series, or a chart axis.

5. *Do any of the following:*
   ▲ Double-click the selected item. An appropriate dialog box appears (**Figure 13.9**), enabling you to edit the item's properties.
   ▲ Choose Format > Selected *item name* or press Ctrl 1 to make the same dialog box appear.
   Set options and click OK.

6. Close the report or form and save the changes.

✔ Tips

■ When the pointer is over a chart element, its name appears as a ScreenTip (**Figure 13.10**).

■ Other edits include changing the chart type, options, or 3D perspective (choose a command from the Chart menu); swapping data rows for columns or vice versa (choose a Data > Series in command); editing chart text; and resizing the chart (return to Design View and drag one of the chart's handles).

■ To change the data displayed in the chart, edit the datasheet.

Creating a PivotTable

A PivotTable is a data display and analysis tool, similar to a crosstab. Unlike a crosstab, however, a PivotTable can easily be modified to show different data groupings. A PivotTable can be based on selected fields from any table, form, or query.

There are several ways to create a PivotTable, but you'll probably find it easiest to use the PivotTable Wizard, as described below.

To create a PivotTable:

1. From the Database window, choose Insert > Form.

   The New Form dialog box appears (**Figure 13.11**).

2. Select PivotTable Wizard. From the drop-down list, select the table or query from which the data will be drawn. Click OK.

3. Read the explanatory text in the new screen, and click OK.

4. In the next screen (**Figure 13.12**), select fields to use in the PivotTable.

   You can include fields from *multiple* tables or queries, if you like. Select another table or query from the drop-down list, select a field, and then click the single arrow button to move the field into the Fields Chosen for Pivoting list.

5. Click Finish.

   A blank PivotTable and PivotTable Field List appear (**Figure 13.13**).

6. Drag fields from the Field List into the PivotTable filter, column, row, and data drop areas (**Figure 13.14**).

7. *Optional:* To switch from raw data to totals, right-click a data heading and choose AutoCalc > Sum from the pop-up menu that appears.

   Totals replace the raw data (**Figure 13.15**).

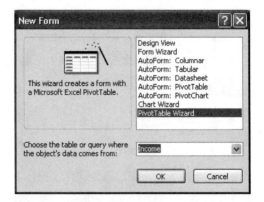

Figure 13.11 Select PivotTable Wizard, and select a table or query as the data source.

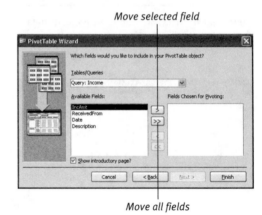

Figure 13.12 Select the fields that you want to use.

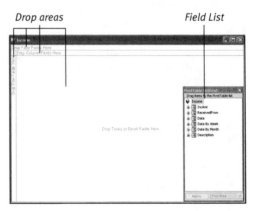

Figure 13.13 Move fields from the Field List into the drop areas.

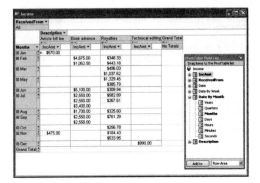

Figure 13.14 A PivotTable and its initial set of fields.

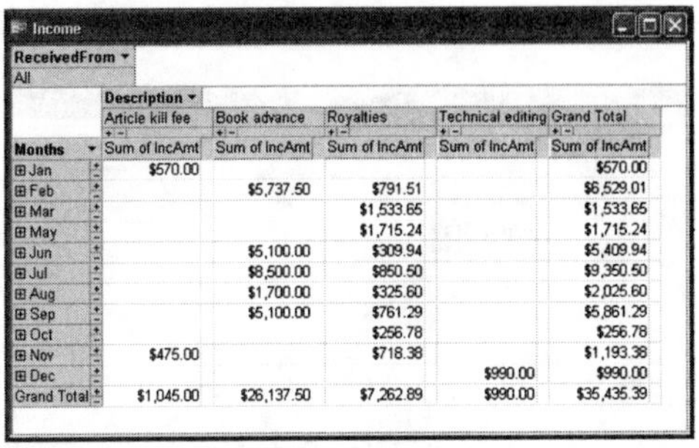

Figure 13.15 To prevent the PivotTable from displaying all of the raw data, you can use a Sum function to present only totals.

Figure 13.16 By clicking an expand indicator, a Date field can be displayed as years, quarters, or months, rather than as full dates.

✔ Tips

■ A PivotTable can also be attached to an *existing* table, form, or query. Rather than creating a new form for the PivotTable, open the appropriate table, form, or query, choose View > PivotTable View, and design the PivotTable. To later view or modify the PivotTable, reopen the original table, form, or query, and choose View > PivotTable View.

■ Some fields in the PivotTable Field List can be expanded to show other variants. A Date field, for example, can be displayed as the full date, a date by week, or a date by month. To display only the names of the months (see Figure 13.14), expand Date By Month in the PivotTable Field List (**Figure 13.16**) and then drag the Months item into the drop area.

■ To eliminate a field, right-click it in the table and choose Remove from the pop-up menu that appears.

Working with PivotTables

Although you can certainly get useful information from static PivotTables, the truly wonderful thing about them is the ease with which they can be rearranged to provide different views of your data. The following list shows some of the ways that you can work with PivotTables.

To work with a PivotTable:

◆ *Do any of the following:*

▲ Click expand indicators (the + icons) to show all data detail.

▲ Rearrange column or row headings by dragging them to new positions. Rather than showing an alphabetical list of departments as column headings, you might want to list them in order of importance or group them by function, for example.

▲ Add additional fields to the column or row drop areas to display subgroups. For instance, moving the ReceivedFrom field into the columns area so it's to the right of Description will result in each income type (such as royalties) being divided among its source companies.

▲ When there are multiple fields in the column or row drop areas, they, too, can be rearranged by dragging to give different views of the data.

▲ You can restrict the data so it shows only selected groups and subgroups. Click a down arrow on the PivotTable (**Figure 13.17**), add or remove checkmarks, and click OK.

▲ You can display totals or other summary statistics rather than raw data. Right-click a raw data element in the table and choose AutoCalc, followed by a summary statistic (such as Sum). You can then collapse each of the row headings to show only the summary statistics (**Figure 13.18**).

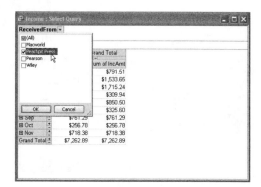

Figure 13.17 To restrict the data to only selected categories, add or remove checkmarks. Click All to check or clear all check boxes.

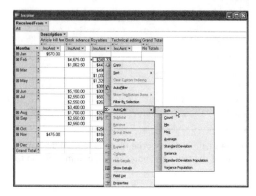

Figure 13.18 You can generate summary statistics by using an AutoCalc function.

Figure 13.19 You can format an item by selecting options from this formatting toolbar.

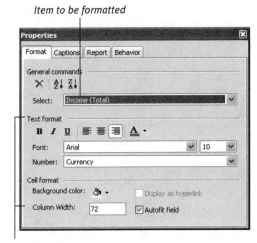

Item to be formatted

Formatting options

Figure 13.20 If you want to alter the formatting of several items, it's more convenient to do so in the Properties dialog box.

Caption text

Figure 13.21 You can edit the Caption text to create more understandable column headings.

Formatting a PivotTable

If you like, you can alter the appearance of any PivotTable. Some properties that you can change include the font, size, style, color, and alignment of text; background colors for table areas; and the text for headings. Note that formatting changes apply to an entire section of the PivotTable, rather than to individual elements.

To format a PivotTable:

◆ *Do any of the following:*

▲ Select a table element and then select settings from the Formatting (PivotTable/PivotChart) toolbar (**Figure 13.19**).

▲ Select a table element, and click the Properties toolbar icon, choose View > Properties, or press Alt Enter. Set new options in the Properties dialog box that appears (**Figure 13.20**).

▲ Right-click a table element and choose Properties from the pop-up menu. Set new options in the Properties dialog box (see Figure 13.20).

✔ Tips

■ When the Properties dialog box opens, it's set to modify the currently selected element. However, you can alter *any* element—regardless of the one that's selected—by selecting its name from the Select drop-down list. Change as many elements as you like and then click the close box.

■ To change a column heading or a field name, select it and then switch to the Captions tab of the Properties dialog box. Edit the Caption text as desired (**Figure 13.21**).

Creating a PivotChart

A PivotChart is the graphic counterpart to a PivotTable. By dragging fields into the drop areas, rearranging them, and setting options, you can create charts that enable you to view your data in many useful ways. Like a Pivot-Table, a PivotChart can be based on selected fields from any table, form, or query.

To create a PivotChart:

1. *Do one of the following:*
   ▲ Open the table, form, or query on which you want to base the PivotChart, and choose View > PivotChart View.
   ▲ From the Database window, choose Insert > Form. In the New Form dialog box, select AutoForm: PivotChart, specify a table or query on which to base the PivotChart, and click OK.

   A blank PivotChart and Chart Field List appear (**Figure 13.22**).

2. *Optional:* By default, Access proposes to create a column chart. If you'd prefer a different type of chart, right-click anywhere in the chart window, choose Chart Type from the pop-up menu, select a new chart type on the Type tab of the Properties window (**Figure 13.23**), and close the Properties window.

   The drop areas presented depend on the selected chart type.

3. Drag fields from the Chart Field List into the drop areas (such as Category, Series, Filter, and Data).

4. *Optional:* To display a chart legend (**Figure 13.24**), click the Show Legend toolbar icon.

✔ Tip

■ You can also create a PivotChart that's based on an existing PivotTable. Open the PivotTable, and choose View > PivotChart View.

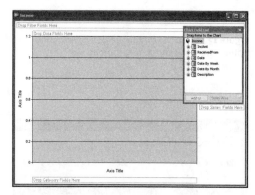

Figure 13.22 When you first create a new PivotChart, a blank chart with designated drop areas is presented.

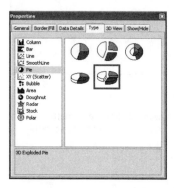

Figure 13.23 You can select a new chart type in this dialog box.

Legend

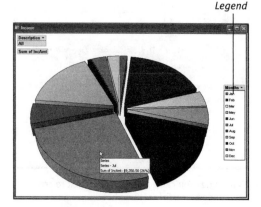

Figure 13.24 Adding a legend makes it simpler to understand the data in your chart.

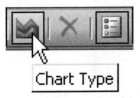

Figure 13.25 When the pointer looks like this, release the mouse button to remove the selected field from the chart.

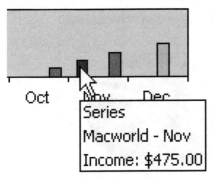

Figure 13.26 Click this icon to change chart types.

Figure 13.27 You can rest the pointer over a data element to learn what it represents.

Working with PivotCharts

Working with a PivotChart is similar to working with a PivotTable, but even simpler. There are fewer options for you to set or change. You can do any of the following with a PivotChart:

◆ You can add additional fields to the drop areas to display subgroups.

◆ When there are multiple fields in a drop area, they can be rearranged by dragging to give different views of the data.

◆ You can restrict the data so it shows only selected groups and subgroups. Click a down arrow, add or remove checkmarks (see Figure 13.17), and then click OK.

◆ To remove a field from a PivotChart, drag it off the chart or into a blank area where the pointer changes to a Delete icon (**Figure 13.25**).

◆ To add or remove the legend, click the Show Legend toolbar icon.

◆ To change chart types, right-click a blank area of the chart, and choose Chart Type from the pop-up menu. You can also click the Chart Type toolbar icon (**Figure 13.26**).

◆ If you close the Chart Field List, you can open it again by clicking the Field List toolbar icon or by choosing View > Field List.

◆ To see the details for any data element, rest the pointer over it for a moment. A ScreenTip will appear (**Figure 13.27**).

Formatting a PivotChart

Formatting a PivotChart is similar to formatting a PivotTable. You can also label axes, add a title, and show or hide the legend.

To format a PivotChart:

◆ *Do any of the following:*

▲ Select a text element and then select settings from the Formatting (PivotTable/PivotChart) toolbar (see Figure 13.19). To delete a text element (such as a title), select it and click the Delete toolbar icon.

▲ Select a chart element, and click the Properties toolbar icon, choose View > Properties, or press ⌈Alt⌉⌈Enter⌉. Set new options in the Properties dialog box that appears.

▲ Right-click a chart element and choose Properties from the pop-up menu. Set new options in the Properties dialog.

▲ To add a title to a chart, click the Add Title icon on the General tab of the Properties dialog box (**Figure 13.28**), switch to the Format tab, and then edit the text in the Caption text box.

▲ You can label an axis by selecting the "Axis Title" text, opening the Properties dialog box, and editing the Caption text (found on the Format tab).

▲ Solid chart elements (such as pie slices and bars) can be shown as solid colors, textures, gradients, or pictures (**Figure 13.29**). Select an element and click the Properties toolbar icon. On the Border/Fill tab of the Properties dialog box, select a new Fill Type and set options for it (**Figure 13.30**).

To use a picture to "color" an element, select Picture/Texture as the Fill Type, click the URL radio button, and then type or paste the picture's Web address or the full path to it on your hard disk.

Click to add a title

Figure 13.28 To add a title to the chart, click the first Add icon.

Texture   Picture   Gradient

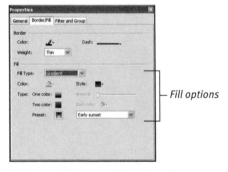

Figure 13.29 Chart elements can also display a texture, picture, or gradient.

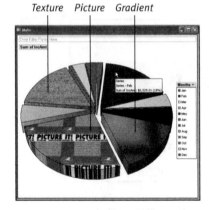

Fill options

Figure 13.30 You can set fill options for a selected element on the Border/Fill tab.

14

CREATING REPORTS

A case can be made that reports are databases' *raison d'être* (reason for existence). Well, perhaps not *the* reason, but certainly one of them.

Reports can help you summarize your data in ways that are impossible by simply scanning through records in a datasheet, form, or query. In addition, reports enable you to share your data with others, including those who wouldn't normally have access to your databases.

Access reports can be created automatically, with the assistance of wizards, or manually in Design View. This chapter concentrates on the first two methods, since this is the easiest way to learn the complexities of creating reports.

In this chapter, you'll learn to do the following:

◆ Create an AutoReport from any table or query.

◆ Use the Label Wizard to create sheets of address labels.

◆ Use the Report Wizard to design an elaborate report with sort fields, grouping levels, and summary statistics.

Creating an AutoReport

An AutoReport is the easiest type of report to create. An AutoReport is a simple report of all fields from a selected table or query, formatted to match the most recent AutoFormat settings and displayed in the current sort order, using the most recent Page Setup settings.

To create an AutoReport:

1. In the Database window, click Reports in the Objects pane.

2. Click the New toolbar icon.

    The New Report dialog box appears (**Figure 14.1**).

3. *Do one of the following:*

    ▲ Select AutoReport: Columnar to arrange records in a vertical stack.

    ▲ Select AutoReport: Tabular to display each record as a row in table format.

4. From the drop-down list, select a table or query on which to base the report and then click OK.

    The report is displayed in a Print Preview window (**Figure 14.2**).

5. Examine the report. If you like, you can click the Setup toolbar icon to alter the Page Setup settings, such as switching the orientation from portrait to landscape.

6. Close the report by clicking the Close toolbar icon or the window's close box.

    A dialog box appears, asking if you'd like to save the report.

7. *Do one of the following:*

    ▲ Click Yes if the report is satisfactory.

    ▲ Click No to discard the report.

    ▲ Click Cancel to continue examining the report in Print Preview mode.

8. If you clicked Yes, name the report in the Save As dialog box that appears, and then click OK.

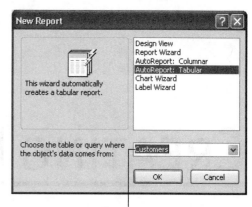

Data source

Figure 14.1 Select an AutoReport format and the table or query from which the data will be drawn.

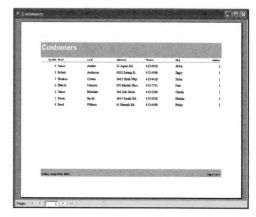

Figure 14.2 An example of an AutoReport: Tabular.

Selected format   Format preview

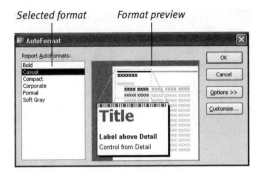

Figure 14.3 Select a new AutoFormat style to be applied to the selected report part(s).

✔ Tips

- If the data source contains many fields, the Tabular format may cause fields to overlap. One possible solution is to use the Page Setup command to switch to landscape mode and then generate the report again.

- While the AutoReport feature works well when based on a table with a limited number of fields, you'll generally get the best results when it's based on a query. Creating a query enables you to select a subset of fields in a particular sort order.

- With many AutoReports, you may find that there are design flaws you still have to correct. For example, fields and labels frequently overlap, you may not care for the overall style of the report, or some fonts may not be to your liking. To make changes to the generated report, switch to Design View and edit it as you would a form. For details, see "Editing Reports," later in this chapter.

- To change the overall style of a report, switch to Design View, choose Edit > Select All, click the AutoFormat toolbar icon, and select another style from the AutoFormat dialog box (**Figure 14.3**).

- To change only one section of a report to another AutoFormat style, switch to Design View, click a part label (such as Report Header or Detail), click the Auto-Format toolbar icon, and select a style from the AutoFormat dialog box (see Figure 14.3).

CREATING AN AUTOREPORT

Creating Labels

Using the Label Wizard, it's incredibly easy to create mailing labels. Unlike the AutoReport wizards, the Label Wizard allows you to select fields and set the label formatting.

To create a label sheet:

1. In the Database window, click Reports in the Objects pane, and click the New icon.

   The New Report dialog box appears (see Figure 14.1).

2. Select Label Wizard, and select the table or query that contains the address data. Click OK to continue.

3. In the next screen (**Figure 14.4**), do the following and then click Next:

   ▲ Select the label manufacturer from the Filter by manufacturer drop-down list.

   ▲ Select a Unit of Measure and a Label Type.

   ▲ Select the label product number from the scrolling list.

4. In the next screen (**Figure 14.5**), set font and style options for the label text. Click Next to continue.

5. In the next screen (**Figure 14.6**), design a single label by moving fields into the Prototype label box. Press [Enter] to end each address line, except the last. Click Next.

   You can insert spaces and punctuation to separate the text elements. You can also add static text (such as *Priority Mail)* by typing it on the prototype label.

6. In the next screen, you can specify one or more fields on which to sort the data.

7. On the final screen, name the label report and click Finish.

   A print preview appears.

8. When finished, close the preview window.

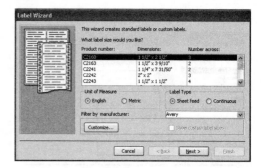

Figure 14.4 Select the label manufacturer and the label's part number.

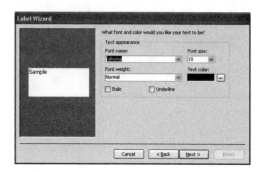

Figure 14.5 Set the font, size, and style for the text.

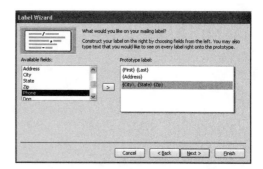

Figure 14.6 Create the layout for the label text. You can include spaces and punctuation to separate the elements.

CREATING LABELS

Select additional tables or queries

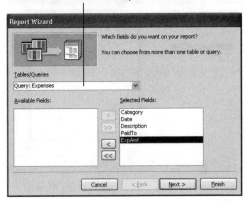

Figure 14.7 Move the desired fields into the Selected Fields list.

Data views   Data grouping preview

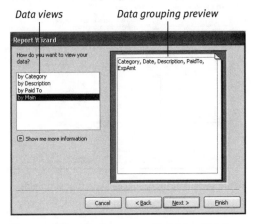

Figure 14.8 Specify the manner (if any) in which the data should be grouped.

Using the Report Wizard

The Report Wizard is a distinct step up from an AutoReport. By selecting options in a series of dialog boxes, you can combine related data from multiple tables, include grouping levels, sort on up to four fields, and choose a layout and style. (Note that statistical summaries are only available if numeric fields are present.)

To create a report using the Report Wizard:

1. In the Database window, click Reports in the Objects pane, and click the New icon.

   The New Report dialog box appears (see Figure 14.1).

2. Select Report Wizard, and select a table or query on which to base the report. Click OK to continue.

   This is merely the *initial* table/query from which you can select fields. In the next step, you can specify additional tables or queries.

3. The fields from the specified table or query are listed on the new screen (**Figure 14.7**). Move fields into the Selected Fields list in the order in which you want them to appear in the report.

4. *Optional:* To include related fields from other tables or queries, choose another table/query from the drop-down list, and then move any desired fields into the Selected Fields list.

5. Click Next to continue.

6. In the next screen (**Figure 14.8**), the wizard suggests possible data groupings that can be created. Select a view and click Next.

   You can either select a grouping arrangement from the list or select a view that offers no grouping. (You can specify a different grouping on the screen that follows.)

   continues on next page

7. In the next screen (**Figure 14.9**), you can add grouping levels to break the data into discrete groups or categories. In a Sales table, for example, the grouping level might be District, Salesperson, or both.

   If setting multiple grouping levels, you can change their priority (moving them up or down) by clicking the Priority buttons.

8. *Optional:* To create groups based on other than the obvious divisions or normal intervals, click the Grouping Options button.

9. Click Next to continue.

10. In the next screen (**Figure 14.10**), you can specify up to four sort fields and orders.

11. *Optional:* If numeric fields were among the selected fields, you can click the Summary Options button to add basic calculations to the report (**Figure 14.11**).

12. Click Next to continue.

13. In the next screen, select a layout style and an orientation for the report. Click Next to continue.

    Optional: Click the Adjust field width check box to force all fields to fit within the width of a single report page. Note, however, that this may result in truncated data and/or column headings.

14. In the next screen, select a report style, and then click Next.

15. In the final screen, enter a name for the report and click Finish.

    The report is added as a new Reports object in the Database window.

✔ Tips

- You can also start the Report Wizard by opening the Reports section of the Database window and double-clicking Create report by using wizard.

- See Chapter 16 for instructions for exporting reports as shareable report snapshots.

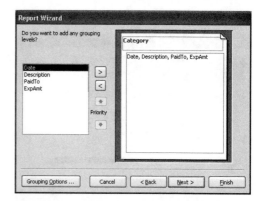

Figure 14.9 If desired, set grouping levels for the report.

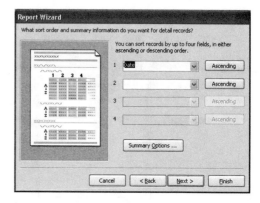

Figure 14.10 If desired, specify up to four sort fields.

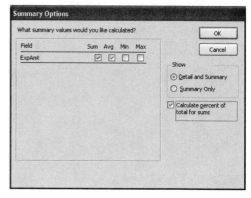

Figure 14.11 You can optionally calculate and display summary statistics for numeric fields.

Clipped heading   Clipped heading

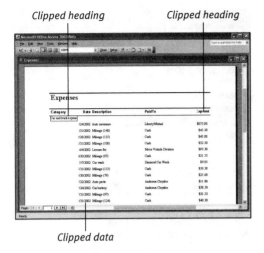

Clipped data

Figure 14.12 Examine your report in the Print Preview window to identify any needed corrections.

Figure 14.13 You use Design View to edit a report.

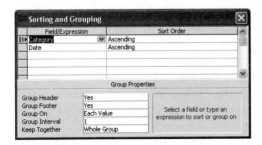

Figure 14.14 Prevent awkward page breaks by setting the Keep Together property to Whole Group.

Editing Reports

If you want to modify a report (whether to pick a different overall style, alter field widths or placement, or set new groupings or sort fields), all changes are made in Design View. If you want to create a report entirely from scratch, you also use Design View.

Assuming that you're working with a wizard-generated report, there are many simple changes you can make to improve a report's appearance. The first step is to examine the output in Print Preview (**Figure 14.12**) or Layout Preview. Look for clipped headings, as well as fields that aren't fully displayed, are unnecessarily wide, or have an undesired alignment. Make any desired changes, moving between Design and Preview views to check their effects. Then save the modified report.

To edit a report:

1. In the Database window, double-click the report that you want to edit.

   The report opens in Print Preview view (see Figure 14.12).

2. Page through the report, noting flaws and other elements that you want to change.

3. Switch to Design View (**Figure 14.13**) by clicking the View toolbar icon.

4. Make any necessary changes, such as the following:

   ▲ Resize, edit, and move headings to make sure that they display fully.

   ▲ Change the font, style, size, and/or color of selected text elements by clicking toolbar icons.

   ▲ Prevent page breaks in the middle of a group. Right-click a blank area and choose Sorting and Grouping from the pop-up menu. Select the main grouping field, and set the Keep Together property to Whole Group (**Figure 14.14**).

continues on next page

5. When you've finished editing the report layout, close its window.

Access asks if you'd like to save the changes to the report's design.

6. Click Yes to save the changes, No to close the file without saving the changes, or Cancel to continue editing the file without closing it.

✔ Tips

■ Examining wizard-generated reports in Design View is one of the easiest ways to learn how to design reports from scratch.

■ When you're designing or editing a report layout, Access offers an additional view that you may find helpful. Choose Layout Preview from the View drop-down list or from the View menu. Rather than displaying all of the detail records, only one is shown per category. In Layout Preview, you can quickly scroll through a report to identify formatting errors.

■ In addition to clicking, you can select an element for editing by choosing its name from the drop-down list on the Formatting (Form/Report) toolbar (**Figure 14.15**).

■ You can move selected elements by dragging or by pressing an arrow key. When Format > Snap to Grid is enabled, movements (whether by dragging or by pressing arrow keys) can only be made to grid intersections.

■ To add a graphic or logo to a report, click the Image icon in the Toolbox and then click the spot in the layout where you want the image to appear, such as in the Report Header.

■ See "Creating an AutoReport" at the beginning of this chapter for help applying an AutoFormat to a section or to the entire report.

Figure 14.15 You can quickly select sections and objects from this drop-down menu.

15

IMPORTING DATA

In Access, *importing* is the process of taking data from a source outside of the current Access database, copying it, and creating a new table from it in the current database. Using the Get External Data command, you can import data from a variety of sources, saving you the time of retyping it. Imported data can become a new table or—with most data types—can be appended to an existing table. You can import data into a new, blank database or into an existing database.

Access also provides another way to share the data of other databases. You can *link* to tables in other databases—without creating a new Access table—and simply read from them as needed.

In this chapter, you'll learn about linking and how to import the following types of data:

- ◆ Paradox and dBASE databases
- ◆ Excel worksheets
- ◆ Microsoft Outlook folders
- ◆ HTML tables
- ◆ Delimited text files
- ◆ Objects from other Access databases

Importing from Paradox and dBASE

Importing from a Paradox or dBASE database is as easy as it gets. All you have to do is specify the database from which you want to import.

To import from Paradox or dBASE:

1. *Do one of the following:*

   ▲ Open an existing database to receive the data as a new table.

   ▲ Create a blank database to receive the data as a new table.

2. Choose File > Get External Data > Import. The Import dialog box appears (**Figure 15.1**).

3. Navigate to the drive and folder that contains the Paradox or dBASE file. From the Files of type drop-down list, select dBASE III, dBASE IV, dBASE 5, or Paradox; select the file; and click Import.

   Access imports the data and creates a table with a name that matches that of the imported file.

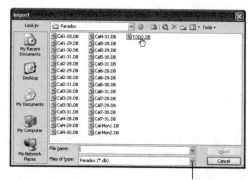

Open the Files of type list

Figure 15.1 Specify the file type of the database to be imported, and then select its name.

After the Import

It's not unusual to have to do some cleanup after importing a new table. For example, some—perhaps many—fields will be the wrong data type. Currency fields are invariably set to Number type, for instance. You may also want to set an input mask for Date/Time fields to ensure that they are displayed correctly. Open the table in Design View and make any necessary changes.

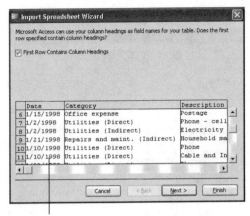

Data preview

Figure 15.2 Indicate whether the first row contains data or column headings (field names).

Create a new table from the data

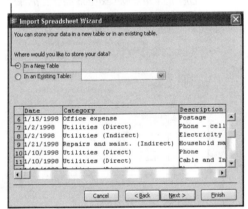

Figure 15.3 Indicate that the data will be imported into a new table.

Importing from Excel

Access can import data from an Excel worksheet, either as a new table or appended onto an existing table. If an Excel 5.0 or higher workbook contains multiple sheets, you can select the one you want to import. For files from Excel 4.0 or earlier, you must resave each sheet in a workbook as a separate file.

To import an Excel worksheet as a new table:

1. *Do one of the following:*
   - ▲ Open an existing database to receive the data as a new table.
   - ▲ Create a blank database to receive the data as a new table.

2. Choose File > Get External Data > Import. The Import dialog box appears (see Figure 15.1).

3. Navigate to the drive and folder that contains the Excel file. Choose Microsoft Excel from the Files of type drop-down list, select the file, and click Import.

   The first screen of the Import Spreadsheet Wizard appears.

4. Check or clear the check box to indicate whether the first row should be treated as data or as column headings (**Figure 15.2**). Click Next to continue.

5. In the next screen (**Figure 15.3**), click the radio button labeled In a New Table, and click Next.

continues on next page

IMPORTING FROM EXCEL

6. In the next screen (**Figure 15.4**), you can edit each field's settings (one by one) by clicking its column and then doing any of the following. Click Next when you're done.

▲ Edit the field's name in the Field Name text box.

▲ Specify whether the field should be indexed and, if so, whether it can contain duplicate values.

▲ Click the Do not import field (Skip) check box to ignore the field when importing the worksheet.

Note that the Data Type box is grayed out. It displays Access' best guess for the data type, based on the data found in the column. If it's incorrect, you can change the data type after the import.

7. In the next screen (**Figure 15.5**), you can create or specify a primary key for the table.

▲ To accept the new ID field as the key, select Let Access add primary key.

▲ To use an existing field as the key, select Choose my own primary key, and select a field from the drop-down list.

▲ To avoid creating or selecting a primary key at this time, select No primary key.

Click Next to continue.

8. In the final screen, enter a name for the new table, and click Finish.

To import an Excel worksheet as appended data:

1. Perform Steps 1–4 from the previous list.

2. In the next screen (see Figure 15.3), click the radio button labeled In an Existing Table, select the table's name from the drop-down list, and click Next.

The final screen appears.

3. Click Finish.

Selected field

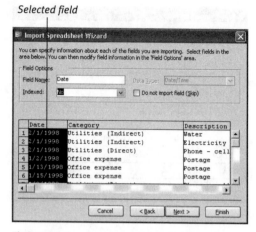

Figure 15.4 To examine or change a field's settings, select it in the preview area. Use the horizontal scroll bar to see fields that are off-screen.

Click here to set an existing field as the key

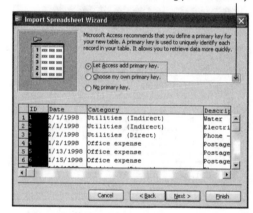

Figure 15.5 Click a radio button to create or select a primary key field for the new table.

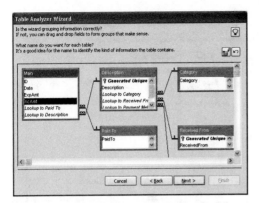

Figure 15.6 With only minor changes, these wizard-suggested tables and relationships are finalized.

✔ Tips

- Since Excel data can be *appended* to a table (rather than creating a new table), you may find it convenient to export other databases to Excel, make any necessary corrections, and then import and append the data into your Access table.

- On the final Import screen, you may want to let the Table Analyzer Wizard (**Figure 15.6**) analyze the imported data. Rather than simply accepting it as a single table, the wizard tries to determine whether a series of related tables would be more efficient—lessening data duplication. If so, the wizard creates the related tables for you, while giving you an opportunity to rename them and reorganize the fields that they contain.

IMPORTING FROM EXCEL

Importing from Outlook

If you use Microsoft Outlook as your email client, you know that it contains a wealth of useful data. Access can import any Outlook folder, including the expansive address book and message folders.

To import data from Outlook:

1. *Do one of the following:*
   - ▲ Open an existing database to receive the data as a new table.
   - ▲ Create a blank database to receive the data as a new table.

2. Choose File > Get External Data > Import. The Import dialog box appears (see Figure 15.1).

3. Choose Outlook from the Files of type drop-down list.
   The Import Exchange/Outlook Wizard appears (**Figure 15.7**).

4. Expand the folders as necessary by clicking the plus (+) icons, select the folder you want to import, and click Next.

5. In the next screen (see Figure 15.3), do one of the following:
   - ▲ To create a new table, click the radio button labeled In a New Table.
   - ▲ To append the data to an existing table, click the radio button labeled In an Existing Table and choose a table from the drop-down list.

   Click Next to continue. (If appending to an existing table, this is the final step.)

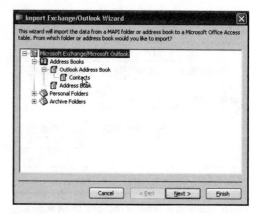

Figure 15.7 Use the Import Exchange/Outlook Wizard to select a folder to import.

6. In the next screen (see Figure 15.4), you can edit each field's settings (one by one) by clicking its column and then doing any of the following. Click Next when you're done.

   ▲ Edit the field's name in the Field Name text box.

   ▲ Change the field's data type.

   ▲ Specify whether the field should be indexed and, if so, whether it can contain duplicate values.

   ▲ Click the Do not import field (Skip) check box to ignore the field when importing the worksheet.

7. In the next screen (see Figure 15.5), you can create or specify a primary key.

   ▲ To accept the new ID field as the key, select Let Access add primary key.

   ▲ To use an existing field as the key, select Choose my own primary key, and select a field from the drop-down list.

   ▲ To avoid creating or selecting a primary key at this time, select No primary key.

   Click Next to continue.

8. In the final screen, enter a name for the new table, and click Finish.

✔ Tip

■ The contents of most Outlook folders can change quickly. If you want the information to always be current, you may prefer to link to the data rather than importing it.

Importing HTML Data

Access can also import data from tables or lists in HTML (Web) pages (**Figure 15.8**). The procedure is fairly simple, although it does require that the Web page reside on disk, rather than on the Internet.

To import data from a Web page:

1. *Do one of the following:*

    ▲ Open an existing database to receive the data as a new table.

    ▲ Create a blank database to receive the data as a new table.

2. Choose File > Get External Data > Import. The Import dialog box appears (see Figure 15.1).

3. Choose HTML Documents from the Files of type drop-down list.

4. Navigate to the drive and folder that contains the HTML file, select the file, and click Import.

    The Import HTML Wizard appears (**Figure 15.9**).

5. Click a radio button to indicate whether you'd like to view embedded HTML tables or lists.

6. Select the desired table or list in the scrolling text box on the right. Click Next.

    Web pages may be composed of multiple tables and/or lists. To find the correct one, select each one in the scrolling list and then examine the data in the preview area.

7. In the next screen (see Figure 15.2), examine the data and indicate whether the first row does or does not contain column headings. Click Next to continue.

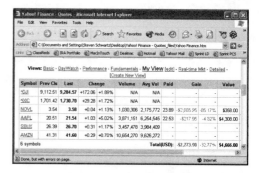

Figure 15.8 You can extract data from Web pages, such as these stock quotes from Yahoo! Finance.

View tables or lists   *Table list*

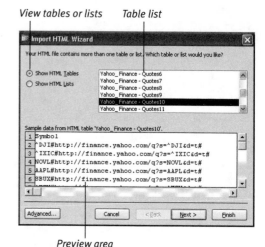

Preview area

Figure 15.9 Indicate whether you want to view lists or tables from the HTML page and then select the correct list or table in the list box. Use the preview area to determine the contents of each table or list.

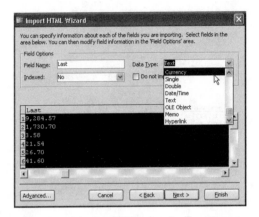

Figure 15.10 Select each field, examine its settings, and fix the incorrect ones, such as changing this data type from Text to Currency.

8. In the next screen (see Figure 15.3), do one of the following:

   ▲ To create a new table, click the radio button labeled In a New Table.

   ▲ To append the data to an existing table, click the radio button labeled In an Existing Table and choose a table from the drop-down list.

   Click Next to continue. (If appending to an existing table, this is the final step.)

9. In the next screen (**Figure 15.10**), you can edit each field's settings (one by one) by clicking its column and then doing any of the following. Click Next when you're done.

   ▲ Edit the field's name in the Field Name text box.

   ▲ Change the field's data type.

   ▲ Specify whether the field should be indexed and, if so, whether it can contain duplicate values.

   ▲ Click the Do not import field (Skip) check box to ignore the field when importing the worksheet.

10. In the next screen (see Figure 15.5), you can create or specify a primary key for the table.

    ▲ To accept the new ID field as the key, select Let Access add primary key.

    ▲ To use an existing field as the key, select Choose my own primary key, and select a field from the drop-down list.

    ▲ To avoid creating or selecting a primary key at this time, select No primary key.

    Click Next to continue.

11. In the final screen, enter a name for the new table, and click Finish.

    The table is added as a new Table object in the Database window.

Importing Text

Many Windows and Macintosh programs, such as databases, spreadsheets, and contact managers, can often save or export their data as a delimited text file. This makes Text an excellent intermediate file format when Access can't read a file in its native format.

Access can import these types of text files:

◆ **Delimited.** A tab, comma, semicolon, space, or other character is used to separate fields. The end of each record is marked by a Return character.

◆ **Fixed width.** Each field is a specific *width* (measured in characters). Unused space at the end of a given field is padded with spaces to fill it out. The end of each record is marked by a Return character.

To import a text file:

1. *Do one of the following:*
   ▲ Open an existing database to receive the data as a new table.
   ▲ Create a blank database to receive the data as a new table.

2. Choose File > Get External Data > Import. The Import dialog box appears (see Figure 15.1).

3. Choose Text Files from the Files of type drop-down list.

4. Navigate to the drive and folder that contains the text file, select the file, and click Import.
   The Import Text Wizard appears (**Figure 15.11**).

5. Click a radio button to indicate whether the data is delimited or fixed width. Click Next.
   Depending on the format selected, **Figure 15.12** (delimited) or **Figure 15.13** (fixed width) appears.

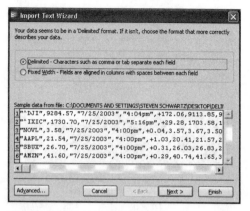

Figure 15.11 The raw data is displayed in the preview area at the bottom of the wizard. Select the appropriate data format: delimited or fixed width.

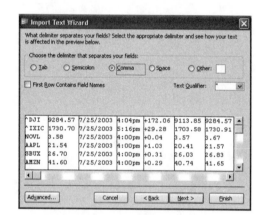

Figure 15.12 When you're working with a delimited text file, this screen appears. As you set options, check the preview area to ensure that the data is represented correctly.

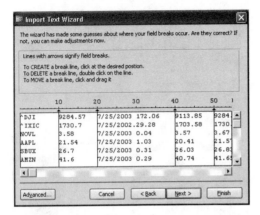

Figure 15.13 When you're working with a fixed width text file, this screen appears. The vertical lines mark the field breaks.

6. *Do one of the following:*

▲ **Delimited.** Select the delimiter character by clicking its radio button or by typing its character in the Other text box. If necessary, select a different *text qualifier* (the character that surrounds text fields). Indicate whether the first row contains field names or data. As you make selections, the preview area shows how the imported data will be formatted.

▲ **Fixed width.** Access displays vertical lines to mark breaks between fields. You can change their positions, add other breaks, or remove breaks, if needed.

Click Next to continue.

7. In the next screen (see Figure 15.3), do one of the following:

▲ To create a new table, click the radio button labeled In a New Table.

▲ To append the data to an existing table, click the radio button labeled In an Existing Table and choose a table from the drop-down list.

Click Next to continue. (If appending to an existing table, this is the final step.)

8. In the next screen (see Figure 15.4), you can edit each field's settings (one by one) by clicking its column and then doing any of the following. Click Next when you're done.

▲ Edit the field's name in the Field Name text box.

▲ Change the field's data type.

▲ Specify whether the field should be indexed and, if so, whether it can contain duplicate values.

▲ Click the Do not import field (Skip) check box to ignore the field when importing the worksheet.

continues on next page

9. In the next screen (see Figure 15.5), you can create or specify a primary key.

▲ To accept the new ID field as the key, select Let Access add primary key.

▲ To use an existing field as the key, select Choose my own primary key, and select a field from the drop-down list.

▲ To avoid creating or selecting a primary key at this time, select No primary key.

Click Next to continue.

10. In the final screen, enter a name for the new table, and click Finish.

The table is added as a new Table object in the Database window.

✔ Tip

■ Many of the Import wizards contain an Advanced button (see Figure 15.12 or 15.13, for example). If you need to repeatedly import a data set in which the format is constant but the data changes, click Advanced to specify importing instructions (**Figure 15.14**) and save them for reuse. When you next import the data set, click Advanced and then click Specs to reload your saved instructions.

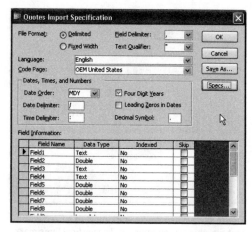

Figure 15.14 Click the Advanced button to open the Import Specification dialog box. You can save settings for reuse (click Save As) or load previously saved settings (click Specs).

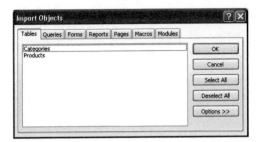

Figure 15.15 When importing from an Access database, you can import multiple objects of various types.

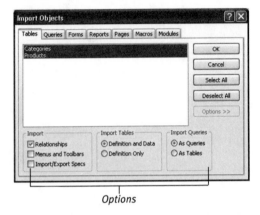

Options

Figure 15.16 By exposing the options section of the dialog box (bottom), you can specify what specific elements of each selected object will be imported.

Importing from Access

You can import data and other objects from Access databases in order to make them part of the current database. For example, if another database contains a table of state names or zip codes, you could import the table and use it as a lookup list in the current database. Access objects that you can import include tables, queries, forms, reports, data access pages, macros, and modules.

To import objects from another Access database:

1. *Do one of the following:*
   - ▲ Open an existing database to receive the data as a new table.
   - ▲ Create a blank database to receive the data as a new table.

2. Choose File > Get External Data > Import. The Import dialog box appears (see Figure 15.1).

3. Choose Microsoft Office Access from the Files of type drop-down list.

4. Navigate to the drive and folder that contains the database, select the file, and click Import.
   The Import Objects dialog box appears (**Figure 15.15**).

5. Click the appropriate tabs and select the object(s) that you want to import.

6. Click the Options button.
   The window expands (**Figure 15.16**), enabling you to view or change the import options.

7. Click OK to perform the import of the selected object(s).

✔ Tip

- ■ Not all imported objects will work as is. For example, reports may refer to data that isn't available in the current database.

Linking to External Data

There are situations where you may prefer to *link* to a table rather than importing it. For example, if the table is regularly changed by others who are using it, linking ensures that you're working with current data. Linking allows you to view, add, and otherwise manipulate the external data (assuming that you have permission). Linking to a table in another database, program (such as Outlook), or file is like working with a relationship. The linked data always resides in the original table, application, or file. Like related data, it is only *displayed* as a table in the current database.

Using the Linked Table Manager, you can force an update of linked tables. This can be helpful if the linked database has been moved to a new location on disk or the network, for instance. You can also break a link between the current database and an external table. You can delete the link (removing the table from the current database) or copy the linked table's structure and/or data to create a new static (unlinked) table in the current database.

To link to an external table:

1. Open a database or create a new database.

2. Choose File > Get External Data > Link Tables.

   The Link dialog box appears, identical in appearance and function to the Import dialog box (see Figure 15.1).

3. If the selected database or file contains multiple tables, you'll be asked to select one.

4. Perform the same steps that you would if importing a table—with the following differences:

   ▲ The linked table will be a new table. You cannot append its data to a table.

   ▲ You cannot modify the linked table's field specifications.

   ▲ You cannot create or modify the table's primary key field.

Figure 15.17 Enter a checkmark for each table that you want to refresh or that may have been moved.

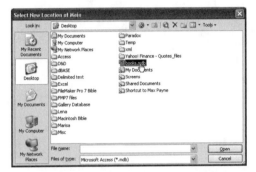

Figure 15.18 If Access notifies you that a given table has been moved, select the table in its new location.

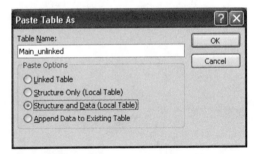

Figure 15.19 Name the new table and specify whether it will be empty or contain a copy of the current data.

To view or refresh links:

1. Open your Access database that contains links. Choose Tools > Database Utilities > Linked Table Manager.

The Linked Table Manager dialog box appears (**Figure 15.17**), displaying the names and locations of all tables that are linked to the current database.

2. Enter a checkmark for each linked table that you want to refresh, and then click OK.

3. If the file containing the linked data has been moved, the Select New Location dialog box appears (**Figure 15.18**). Locate the file, select it, and then click Open.

If you or Access cannot locate the file, the refresh will not occur.

To break a link with an external table:

◆ *Do one of the following:*

▲ Select the table's name in the Database window and press Delete. Note that this doesn't affect the external table; it merely breaks the link to it, removing it from the current database.

▲ Select the table's name in the Database window, choose Edit > Copy (Ctrl C), and choose Edit > Paste (Ctrl V). In the Paste Table As dialog box (**Figure 15.19**), name the new table, select Structure Only (Local Table) or Structure and Data (Local Table), and click OK. You can now select the linked table's name in the Database window and remove it by pressing Delete.

LINKING TO EXTERNAL DATA

16

EXPORTING DATA

Exporting is the process of transferring a copy of data to a new file—typically in a different file format. Your reason for exporting data may be one of the following:

◆ You need to perform additional analyses that are not possible in the original application (in this case, Access).

◆ You want to make your data available to someone who uses a different application.

◆ You (or your company) are switching to a different application, but want to be able to reuse your existing data.

Access can export data in a variety of ways and output it in several popular formats. In this chapter, I'll cover the export procedures and options that you are most likely to use, including the following:

◆ Exporting an entire data table or selected records to another Windows application, such as Microsoft Excel

◆ Exporting data to a text file, enabling it to be read by virtually *any* program

◆ Exporting data to XML *(Extensible Markup Language)*

◆ Exporting data and other Access objects, so they can be used in a *different* Access database

For information on exporting data to the Web, see Chapter 17.

Preparing to Export Data

First, the good news. It's easy to export an entire table to any supported file format. Most export formats also enable you to export only selected records from a given table by first filtering the data. Furthermore, you can also sort the data and omit selected fields.

Now, here's the bad news. Access isn't consistent in the manner in which these things are done. And for some export formats, these additional options aren't available. Here are some general tips to help in the export process:

◆ If you want to export only a subset of records, have the exported data sorted in a given order, or only include specific fields, you must prepare the datasheet prior to issuing the Export command.

◆ To export a subset of records, you can manually select contiguous records (**Figure 16.1**) or use one of the commands in the Records > Filter submenu (**Figure 16.2**), as explained in Chapter 10.

◆ To exclude some fields from the export, use the Format > Hide Columns command or manually hide the columns.

◆ To utilize a table's new sort order (see Chapter 9) or hidden columns (see Chapter 5), be sure to check the Save Formatted check box in the Export Table dialog box.

◆ You cannot export a *subdatasheet* (related data displayed in the current table, as shown in **Figure 16.3**). Export it separately from its actual table.

◆ You may sometimes find it simpler to export the results of a query than to export from a table. If you modify the query by sorting the results or rearranging the columns, for example, you must Save before performing the export.

Record selector

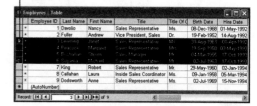

Figure 16.1 To select a record subset, start by clicking a record selector. Then drag up or down to select the additional records or [Shift]-click the final record.

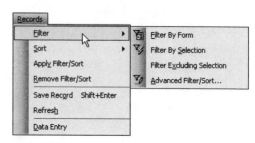

Figure 16.2 Another way to select a record subset is to filter the table to display only the desired records.

Subdatasheet

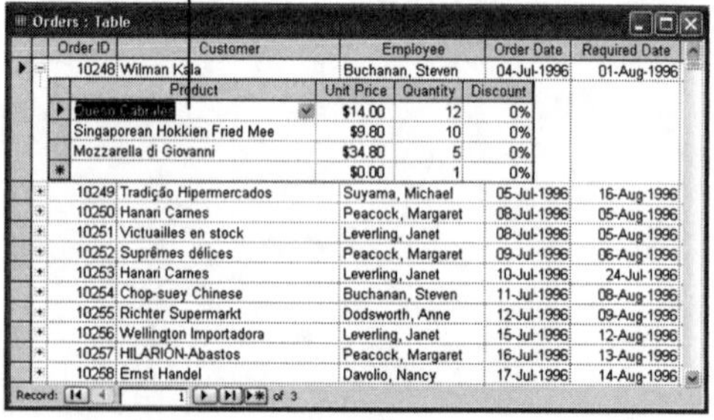

Figure 16.3 Although a subdatasheet is *displayed* as though it's part of this table, the data never leaves its original table. To export its data, do so from its actual table.

Objects pane   Selected table

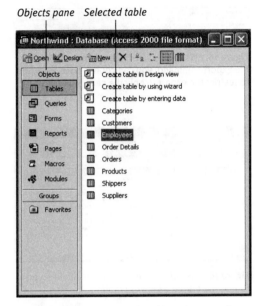

Figure 16.4 Click Tables in the Objects pane, and then select or open the table that you want to export.

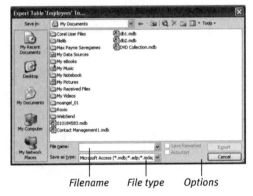

Filename   File type   Options

Figure 16.5 Specify an export file type, name, and other options in the Export Table dialog box.

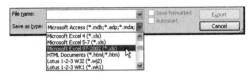

Figure 16.6 Choose an export file type or format from this drop-down list in the Export Table dialog box.

Exporting Data to Another Program

You may want to export your Access data to another program so you can do one of the following:

◆ Allow your data to be read and integrated into a *foreign* (non-Access) database.

◆ Create Excel charts based on the data or perform analyses that would be cumbersome or impossible with Access.

To export a complete, unaltered table:

1. Open the database in Access.

2. *Do one of the following:*

   ▲ In the Database window, select the table you want to export (**Figure 16.4**).

   ▲ Open the table's datasheet by double-clicking the table name in the Database window.

3. Choose File > Export.

   The Export Table *'table name'* To dialog box appears (**Figure 16.5**).

4. Select a file type (such as Microsoft Excel 97-2002) from the Save as type drop-down list (**Figure 16.6**).

   The table's name is proposed as the filename, but with an extension that matches the selected export file type.

5. *Optional:* Select a different destination folder and edit the proposed filename.

6. Click the Export (or Export All) button.

   The export file is created. Any modifications made to the table prior to exporting (such as setting a new sort order or hiding columns) are ignored.

To export a modified table or a subset of records:

1. Open the database in Access.

2. Open the datasheet for the table by double-clicking the table's name in the Database window.

3. Modify the table as desired by doing any of the following:

   ▲ Select a record subset by filtering or drag-selecting.

   ▲ Sort the table by one or several fields.

   ▲ Hide fields that you don't want to export.

4. Choose File > Export.

   The Export Table *'table name'* To dialog box appears (see Figure 16.5).

5. Select a file type from the Save as type drop-down list.

   The table name is proposed as the filename.

6. *Optional:* Select a different destination folder and edit the proposed filename.

7. Click the Save formatted check box.

8. *Optional:* To automatically open the export file in the destination program, click the Autostart check box.

9. *Do one of the following:*

   ▲ To export all displayed records, click the Export (or Export All) button.

   ▲ To export only the currently *selected* records, click the down arrow beside the Export All button and choose Save Selection (**Figure 16.7**).

✔ Tips

■ Exporting to an Office format (Excel or Rich Text Format) provides the most formatting options.

■ Selecting Rich Text Format (RTF) creates a Word table (**Figure 16.8**).

Figure 16.7 When you select records prior to issuing the Export command, you can choose Save Selection to restrict the export to only the selected records.

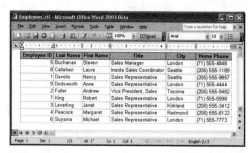

Figure 16.8 Select Rich Text Format as the file type to format the output as a Word table.

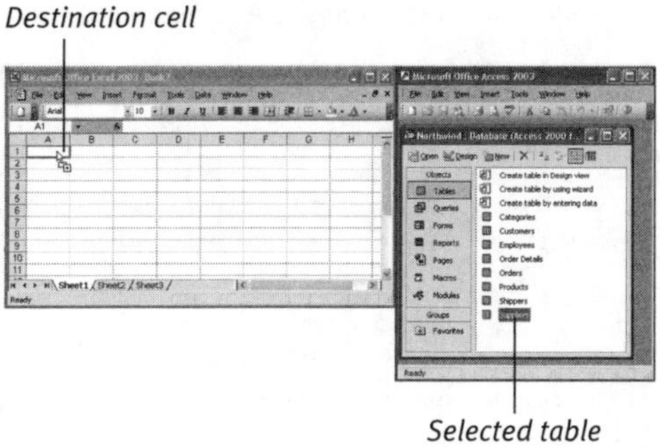

Destination cell

Selected table

Figure 16.9 Select the table in the Database window and then drag it to the destination cell in the Excel worksheet.

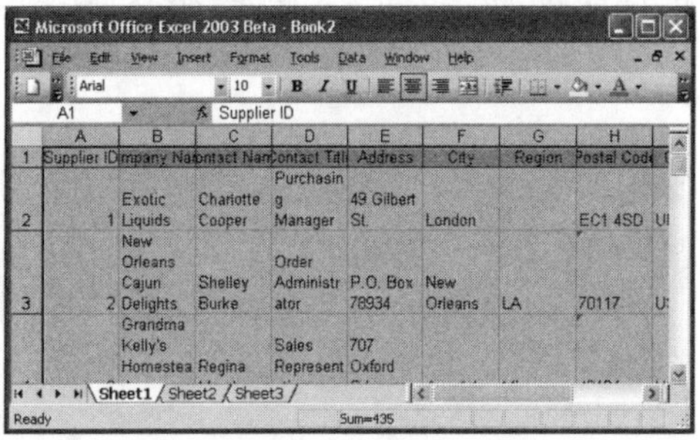

Figure 16.10 When you release the mouse button, a copy of the data appears in the worksheet.

✔ Tips

- When using drag and drop to copy a table into Excel, you can choose *any* destination cell—depending on where you want the table to appear in the worksheet. Be careful not to choose a cell range that already contains data. Doing so will cause the range to be overwritten by the new data.

- You can use drag and drop or the Tools > Office Links > Publish It with Microsoft Word command to export data as a new table in a Word document.

- Access data can also be exported to many Windows applications (such as Excel, Word, or WordPad) via a routine copy-and-paste.

Exporting Data to Excel

Access offers two additional ways to export data to Excel: using drag and drop and the Office Links command. Drag and drop can only be used to copy an entire datasheet into Excel, while Office Links can copy either an entire datasheet or selected records and fields.

To export data to Excel using drag and drop:

1. Open the Access datasheet and launch Excel.

2. An Excel worksheet must be available to receive the data. Do one of the following:

   ▲ If necessary, create a new, blank worksheet using the File > New command.

   ▲ If you want to append the Access data to an existing worksheet, open it now.

3. Arrange and resize the Access and Excel windows so that both are visible.

4. In the Database window, select the table to export, and drag it to the starting cell where you want the data to appear (**Figure 16.9**), such as A1. Release the mouse button.

   The table data appears in the worksheet (**Figure 16.10**).

To export data to Excel using the Office Links command:

1. *Do one of the following:*

   ▲ To export an entire, unmodified table to Excel, click the Tables object in the Database window, and then select the name of the table you want to export.

   ▲ To export a modified table to Excel, open its datasheet and make the desired modifications, such as sorting, hiding columns, and selecting records.

2. Choose Tools > Office Links > Analyze It with Microsoft Excel.

   Access creates a worksheet with the same name as the table, saves, and then opens it.

Exporting Data to a Text File

Exporting data to a text file is an excellent option—and often the *only* one—when you want to reuse your data in a program that can't import Access data and when Access can't export to that program's file type. Almost every database, spreadsheet, and word processing application can read a text file.

Text data can be exported in two formats. In a *delimited text file,* a special character (such as a tab or comma) is used to separate the fields within each record. In a *fixed-width text file,* every field has a set width (in characters). Data in a given field is padded with spaces as needed to achieve the field's preset width.

To export data as a delimited text file:

1. In the Database window, select the table that you want to export or open the table's datasheet by double-clicking its name.

2. Choose File > Export.

   The Export Table *'table name'* To dialog box appears (see Figure 16.5).

3. Select Text Files from the Save as type drop-down list (see Figure 16.6).

4. *Optional:* Select a different destination folder and edit the proposed file name.

5. Click the Export (or Export All) button.

   The Export Text Wizard appears (**Figure 16.11**).

6. Ensure that the Delimited radio button is selected and then click Next.

7. Select a field delimiter and a *text qualifier* (the character that will surround each Text field), as shown in **Figure 16.12.**

8. *Optional:* Click the Include Field Names on First Row check box.

   This option creates a first record that contains the names of the fields being exported.

9. Click the Next button, and then Finish.

File formatting options   Preview area

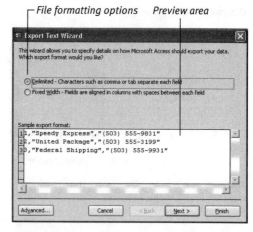

Figure 16.11 Select a data format in the initial screen of the Export Text Wizard. The preview area shows the results of the current choices on your actual data.

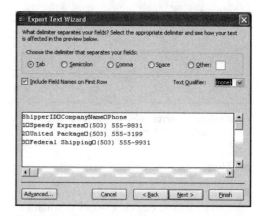

Figure 16.12 Select characters for the field delimiter and the text qualifier. You can optionally output a list of field names as the initial export record.

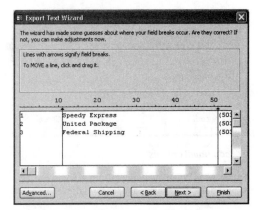

Figure 16.13 Move the dividing lines to set the field widths. Be sure to scroll through all records to ensure that you aren't truncating the data in any field.

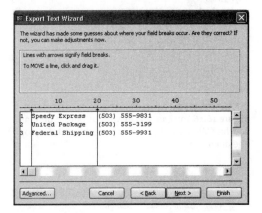

Figure 16.14 These are the revised field widths.

To export data as a fixed-width file:

1. Perform Steps 1–5 of the previous step list.

2. Click the Fixed Width radio button (see Figure 16.11), and then click Next.

   Access displays the proposed field widths (**Figure 16.13**).

3. Adjust the field widths by dragging the field dividing lines to new positions (**Figure 16.14**).

4. Click Next, and then click Finish.

   The fixed-width text file is generated.

✔ Tips

■ Try to select a delimiter character that isn't used within the field data. The tab character is usually a safe choice.

■ "None" is often the best choice for the Text Qualifier. Most programs don't strip the embedded text qualifiers from your exported data. Quotation marks are frequently interpreted as being part of the field data; you will have to manually delete them.

■ When selecting a delimiter and text qualifier, consult the receiving program's manual. If you're unsure, set them to Tab and None.

■ Unless you're sure that the receiving application can't interpret the first record as field names, click the Include Field Names on First Row check box. You can later delete this record if it is interpreted as data, rather than as field names.

■ If you export a subset of records, sorted, and/or with hidden columns, you will not be allowed to set other text file options (such as the delimiter to use). That is, the Export Text Wizard will not appear. In the Export Table dialog box, click the Save formatted check box, and either click Export All (to export the entire table) or Save Selection (to export only the selected records).

Exporting Data as XML

In recent years, XML (*Extensible Markup Language*) has become an increasingly popular method of exchanging data among disparate applications. An XML data file contains the data *and* a description of what the data represents. Formatting instructions can be added by applying an XSL (*Extensible Stylesheet Language*) style sheet to the file.

To export data as XML:

1. In the Database window, select the table that you want to export or open the table's datasheet by double-clicking its name.

2. Choose File > Export.

   The Export Table *'table name'* To dialog box appears (see Figure 16.5).

3. Select XML Documents from the Save as type drop-down list (see Figure 16.6).

4. *Optional:* Select a different destination folder and edit the proposed filename.

5. Click the Export (or Export All) button.

   The Export XML dialog box appears (**Figure 16.15**).

6. Depending on the boxes checked, Access will export the data, its schema, and/or its presentation.

7. *Optional:* To set additional data, schema, and presentation options, click the Advanced button.

   A tabbed version of the Export XML dialog box appears (**Figure 16.16**). Change the settings as desired.

8. Click OK.

   The XML and related files are generated.

✔ Tip

■ Many applications can open or import XML files. For example, you can open the resulting XML file in Excel (**Figure 16.17**).

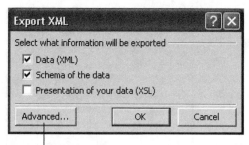

Set additional options

Figure 16.15 When creating XML output, you can export data, its schema, and/or formatting.

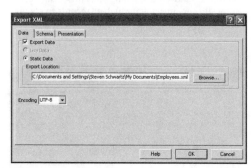

Figure 16.16 You can specify various output options for the XML export by clicking the tabs at the top of the dialog box.

Figure 16.17 This is the Employees XML file, opened in Excel as an XML list.

Table name

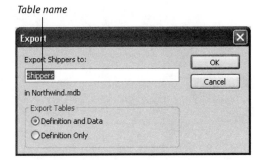

Figure 16.18 When exporting an Access table to another database, you can export both its definition and data or just its definition.

Exporting Data and Objects to Access

If you're developing your own Access databases, you can export any Access object—including tables and their data—to a new file, enabling them to be reused. If, for example, you've created a lengthy list of values that displays as a lookup list when you click into a field, you can export their table and then use it for the same purpose in a new database.

To export an Access table to Access:

1. In the Database window, select the icon for the table that you want to export.

2. Choose File > Export.
   The Export Table *'table name'* To dialog box appears (see Figure 16.5).

3. Ensure that Microsoft Access is selected as the Save as type, and then navigate to the drive and folder in which the destination database is located.

4. Click the destination database's filename, or select it and click the Export button.
   The Export dialog box appears (**Figure 16.18**).

5. Click a radio button to indicate whether you want to export the table definition and its data or only the table definition.

6. *Optional:* Rename the table, if you like.

7. Click OK.
   The table is added as a new object to the destination database.

✔ Tips

■ The procedure for exporting any other type of Access object is identical to that for exporting a table, except that Step 5 is omitted.

■ Access provides other ways to reuse or share objects among databases. First, you can import the necessary objects or tables. Second, you can create active *links* between databases, enabling one database to draw data from another on the same machine or from one accessible over a network. The advantage of linking is that the data is always up-to-date, rather than being a static copy acquired via importing or exporting. Linking to and importing from Access databases are discussed in Chapter 15.

17

ACCESS ON THE WEB

Not everyone you might want to share your data with will own Access. In recent years, Access has provided several ways to make its data available over the Internet and via corporate intranets. In this chapter, you will learn to:

◆ Export a datasheet, form, query, or report as a static HTML table for the Web (viewable with most current browsers).

◆ Publish an Access report as a report snapshot (viewable using Snapshot Viewer, a utility included with Office and as a free download from Microsoft's Web site).

◆ Publish a table as an interactive, online database called a *data access page* (also accessible using a browser).

Creating a Static Web Page

The simplest way to create a Web page from data is to export it as an HTML file. HTML is the language used to create Web pages. When you export a data table, selected records, or selected records and selected fields as HTML, they are displayed as a spreadsheet-style grid—very similar to a datasheet. The resulting file can be uploaded to a Web server or an intranet.

To create a Web page from Access data:

1. Open the datasheet, form, query, or report that you want to export to HTML.

2. *Optional:* Select the specific records and/or fields that you want to export.

   You can filter the data set or—if you're working in a datasheet—drag-select the data that you want to include.

3. *Optional:* Sort the data in the desired order.

4. Choose File > Export.

   An Export dialog box appears.

5. Choose HTML Documents from the Save as type drop-down list (**Figure 17.1**).

6. Access proposes the object name as the HTML filename. You can change it, if you wish.

7. Navigate to the drive and folder in which you want to save the resulting file(s).

8. To create formatted output (rather than using the default style), click the Save formatted check box.

   Some HTML files, such as those generated from reports, already have this option checked. To export selected data, you *must* check this option.

9. *Optional:* To immediately view the output in your default Web browser, click the Autostart check box.

Figure 17.1 In the Export dialog box, select HTML Documents as the file type.

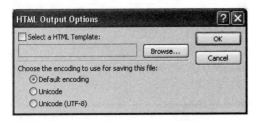

Figure 17.2 Choose this option to export only the selected data.

Figure 17.3 This dialog box is presented if you are creating formatted HTML output or working with selected data.

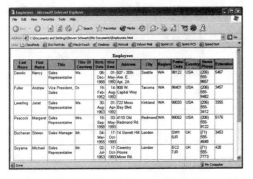

Figure 17.4 An example of formatted output.

Figure 17.5 An example of unformatted output.

10. *Do one of the following:*

▲ To export all records in the default format, click Export All.

▲ To export a report, click Export.

▲ To export only the currently selected records/data subset, click the down arrow beside the Export All button and choose Save Selection (**Figure 17.2**).

11. If you checked the Save formatted check box, the HTML Output Options dialog box appears (**Figure 17.3**).

▲ To alter the format of the output by applying an HTML template to the data, click the check box and click Browse to select the formatting template from your disk. (This assumes that you have or are able to create the template.)

▲ If the output will include foreign language characters, select a Unicode encoding. Otherwise, Default encoding will usually suffice.

Click OK. The HTML output is saved to disk. If there are multiple pages (as there often are in reports), numbered HTML files are saved—one per page. If Autostart was specified in Step 9, the result is displayed in your browser (**Figure 17.4**).

✔ Tips

■ If you didn't select Autostart, you can open the unformatted table (**Figure 17.5**) in any browser by clicking the new HTML file's icon.

■ As mentioned in Step 11, you can create an HTML template file to format your data table. For instructions and an example, see "About the types of Web pages Access creates" in Microsoft Office Access Help.

■ A distinct advantage of exporting to HTML is that virtually every computer user has a browser. You can even email the resulting files to others, if you'd rather not publish them on the Web.

Creating a Report Snapshot

Although you can generate a static HTML page from any report (as described in the previous section), if you want to preserve its appearance, you'll be happier with a report snapshot. Report snapshots are designed to be viewed with Snapshot Viewer, an Office utility program that is installed the first time you create a snapshot. It's also available for free from http://office.microsoft.com/Downloads.

To create a report snapshot:

1. Open the prepared Access report from which you want to create a snapshot (**Figure 17.6**).

2. Choose File > Export.

   An export dialog box appears (see Figure 17.1).

3. Choose Snapshot Format from the Save as type drop-down list.

4. Access proposes the report name as the filename. You can change it, if you wish.

5. Navigate to the drive and folder in which you want to save the resulting file(s).

6. *Optional:* To immediately view the output in Snapshot Viewer, click the Autostart check box.

7. Click the Export button.

   If Autostart was specified in Step 6, the result is displayed in Snapshot Viewer (**Figure 17.7**).

✔ Tip

- For simpler distribution of Access reports, you may want to consider using Adobe Acrobat (www.adobe.com) to generate PDF files from your report snapshots. While many people may not have a copy of Snapshot Viewer, almost *everyone* will have Acrobat Reader/Adobe Reader (the free program used to read PDF files).

Figure 17.6 Open the report in Access.

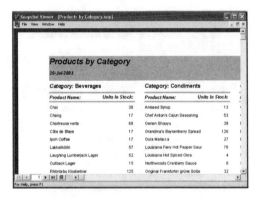

Figure 17.7 Viewing a report in Snapshot Viewer is very much like doing so in Access. The bottom of the window even includes the familiar navigation buttons.

Reports by Email

A report snapshot is just an ordinary file that, as such, can be emailed. You can add the file as a message attachment in your regular email program (such as Microsoft Outlook). Or you can open the snapshot in Snapshot Viewer and choose File > Send.

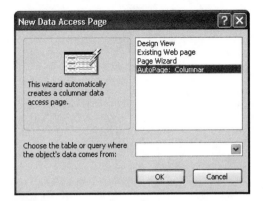

Figure 17.8 You can create a data access page by selecting a method and fields in this dialog box.

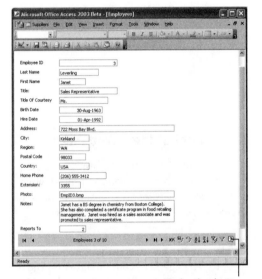

Navigation buttons

Figure 17.9 In a data access page, familiar navigation buttons under each record enable users to navigate among records; create, delete, and save records; sort data; and apply filters.

Creating Data Access Pages

Unlike static Web pages and report snapshots, data access pages are *live*. That is, their data is drawn directly from an Access database. As such, there's no need to worry that you're viewing outdated information—it's *always* up-to-date.

Access provides four ways for you to create a data access page: using the Page Wizard, modifying an existing HTML file, manually designing the page in Design View, or using the AutoPage feature to generate a columnar page from all data in a table or query result. Using AutoPage (described below) is the simplest way to create a data access page.

To create an AutoPage data access page:

1. In the Database window, click the Pages object.

2. Click the New toolbar icon.
   The New Data Access Page dialog box appears (**Figure 17.8**).

3. In the list box, select AutoPage: Columnar.

4. From the drop-down list at the bottom of the dialog box, select a table or query on which to base the new data access page.

5. Click OK.
   Access generates the data access page and displays it in a new window (**Figure 17.9**).

6. To create an HTML page from the data access page, click the Save toolbar icon, choose File > Save, or press Ctrl S. In the Save As Data Access Page dialog box, navigate to the desired drive and folder, edit the proposed filename (if you wish), and click Save.

7. To see how the page looks and functions in a Web browser, choose File > Web Page Preview. (As explained in Step 6, the page *must* be saved as an HTML file before it can be viewed in a browser.)

continues on next page

✔ Tips

- To make a data access page available to other users, you must publish it to a Web server (either on the Internet or an intranet). The actual Access database must also be available—either on a server or a shared computer. Because the link to the database is generated at the same time as the data access page, it will be simpler if you move the database to the server or shared computer *before* creating the data access page.

- To connect to a data access page, each user must have Microsoft Office installed on his or her computer (or have a valid Office license).

- There are no built-in data access page features for ensuring the security of the Web pages or preventing unauthorized changes to the underlying Access tables. If security is a consideration (and it will be, if the page is available on the Internet), you may want to designate the pages and/or the database as read-only. You can also employ other measures, such as setting user-level security (via passwords) for the generated data access pages. For more information, refer to "About securing a data access page" in Microsoft Office Access Help.

- To create a data access page that displays only selected fields, use the Page Wizard (see Figure 17.8). Using this method, you can also present fields from *multiple* tables and/or queries.

- Changes to the Web data access page and to the underlying database are communicated when a changed record is saved. If you think you're viewing out-of-date data on the Web page, click the browser's Refresh (or Reload) toolbar icon.

Publishing a Web Page

If you have a Web site or access to space on your ISP's Web server, you can publish your static Web page, report snapshot, or data access page—enabling others to view it.

Generally, the process involves using an FTP (File Transfer Protocol) utility to upload your Web page(s) to your directory on the Web server. For example, if I created a Web page named sales.htm and placed it in the main directory of my site, it could be viewed online by entering the following address in a Web browser:

http://www.siliconwasteland.com/sales.htm

To publish a report snapshot, upload the .snp file to the Web site and add a link to the file on one of your Web pages. When anyone clicks the link, the file will download to their computer.

SECURITY AND MAINTENANCE

18

If your data is important to you, you'll want to pay special attention to the material in this chapter. Here you'll learn to perform the following maintenance and security tasks:

- Backing up a database
- Compacting and repair a database
- Password-protecting a database
- Establishing user-level security for a database

Backing Up a Database

It's vital that you routinely make backup copies of your databases. In the event that the original database is damaged, you can restore the most recent backup copy.

To make a backup copy of a database:

1. Open the database if it isn't already open.

2. Close all database objects and save them to preserve any changes made in the current session.

   The only item that should remain open is the Database window.

3. Choose File > Back Up Database or Tools > Database Utilities > Back Up Database.

   The Save Backup As dialog box appears (**Figure 18.1**).

4. Navigate to the drive and folder in which you want to store the backup file.

5. Access proposes the original filename, plus today's date as the name for the new backup file (*Sales_2003-07-21.mdb*, for example). If you like, you can edit the name.

6. Click Save to create the backup.

✔ Tips

■ To restore a backup, copy it to the desired folder (such as the folder in which the database it will replace is stored). After copying the file, rename it to match the original filename.

   To rename a file, right-click its file icon and choose Rename from the pop-up menu that appears.

■ You can also use Windows to create a backup. Open the database's folder, right-click its file icon, and drag it onto or into the destination folder. When you release the mouse button, choose Copy Here from the pop-up menu appears (**Figure 18.2**).

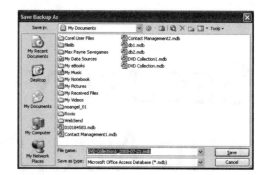

Figure 18.1 Name the backup, choose a destination for it, and click Save.

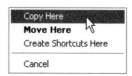

Figure 18.2 To create the copy, choose Copy Here.

Create a Backup Strategy

Unless all you're interested in preserving is a database's design, one backup won't do the trick. In most cases, you'll want *multiple* backups. The frequency with which you back up a database should be determined by:

◆ The frequency with which the data or the database design changes

◆ The amount of data and design changes that you can afford to lose

For an infrequently used single-user database, it may suffice to back up only after each significant data entry session. On the other hand, critical company databases are often backed up daily, several times per day, or even hourly.

Depending on a database's importance, it's also wise to regularly *archive* a backup copy. Once a week or month, back up the database to CD, DVD, or tape, and then store the copy off-site for safekeeping.

BACKING UP A DATABASE

Figure 18.3 Select the database that you want to compact or repair.

Figure 18.4 You can save the compacted file using a different name or in another location. (To overwrite the original database, select its file name.)

Compacting and Repairing a Database

Every Access database—no matter how many fields, records, tables, and other objects it contains—is stored on disk as a single file. As you use the database, the process of adding, deleting, and editing records creates wasted space in the file. By periodically using the Compact and Repair Database command, you can reduce the file's size and eliminate the wasted space. And if a database is damaged, the same command can be used to repair it.

To compact/repair an open database:

◆ Choose Tools > Database Utilities > Compact and Repair Database.

The file is checked for errors, compacted, and then replaced with the compacted version. When the process is completed, the database automatically reopens.

To compact/repair a closed database:

1. If a database is currently open, close it now.

2. Choose Tools > Database Utilities > Compact and Repair Database.

The Database to Compact From dialog box appears (**Figure 18.3**).

3. Navigate to the drive and folder that contains the database, and select its name from the file list.

An identical dialog box named Compact Database Into appears (**Figure 18.4**).

4. Navigate to the drive and folder in which you want to store the compacted database.

To replace the database with its compacted version, use the original folder.

continues on next page

5. *Do one of the following:*

   ▲ Accept the proposed name for the compacted file that's presented in the File name text box.

   ▲ Replace the proposed name with one of your choosing.

   ▲ Select the original filename from the file list (to replace the database with the compacted file).

6. If you're replacing the original database with the compacted file, a confirmation dialog box will appear (**Figure 18.5**). Click Yes.

   or

   Click the Save button.

   The database is compacted/repaired and saved to the specified filename and location on disk.

✔ Tips

■ Microsoft recommends that you regularly compact your databases. Rather than rely on your memory, you can instruct Access to automatically compact a given database by choosing Tools > Options, clicking the General tab in the Options dialog box that appears (**Figure 18.6**), and clicking the Compact on Close check box.

■ To compact a shared database, all users must close it before the compacting procedure can begin.

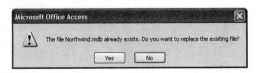

Figure 18.5 Click Yes to replace the original database with the compacted/repaired one, or click No to cancel the procedure.

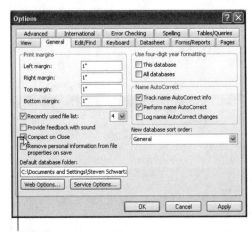

Compact whenever the file is closed

Figure 18.6 To automate the compacting procedure, click the Compact on Close check box.

Figure 18.7 This dialog box appears when you try to open a password-protected database.

About Data Security

With the advent of networks—especially those that are accessible via the Internet—security has become an important consideration for any business. Corporate databases often contain sensitive information that could be disastrous for a business if it found its way into the wrong hands. Access has two features that can help protect a database from prying eyes:

◆ **Password.** You can assign a single password to a database that must be supplied each time it is opened (**Figure 18.7**). Any user who knows the password is granted full access to the data and objects. However, the password is stored in unencrypted form, allowing it to be discovered by anyone with the necessary software tools. Password protection is best applied to single-user databases, rather than to multiuser (shared) databases.

◆ **User-level security.** This is Access' more sophisticated form of database protection. By assigning users to groups and giving them passwords, you can specify the tables, forms, queries, reports, and macros they will be allowed to access. You can also specify the types of *permissions* that each user or group has. For instance, you might set a form as read-only for a given user or group, preventing the person(s) from modifying the data.

✔ Tip

■ Regardless of the type of security measures you employ, be sure to create an unprotected backup copy of the database before adding a password or user-level security.

Password-Protecting a Database

Assigning a password is a simple way to provide basic security for a database.

To assign a password to a database:

1. Open the database.

2. Choose Tools > Security > Set Database Password.

   The Set Database Password dialog box appears (**Figure 18.8**).

3. Enter the same password in both text boxes, and then click OK.

   Letter case makes a difference. For example, *rabbit7* and *Rabbit7* are not equivalent.

To remove a password from a database:

1. Choose File > Open or press Ctrl O.
   The Open dialog box appears.

2. Navigate to the drive and folder that contains the database from which you want to remove the password.

3. Click an empty spot in the dialog box, and select the database's filename by pressing ↓ and ↑.

4. Click the down arrow beside the Open button, and choose Open Exclusive (**Figure 18.9**).

   The Password Required dialog box appears (see Figure 18.7).

5. Enter the password and click OK.
   The database opens.

6. Choose Tools > Security > Unset Database Password.

   The Unset Database Password dialog box appears (**Figure 18.10**).

7. Enter the password and click OK.
   The password protection is eliminated.

Figure 18.8 To create a password, you must enter it twice.

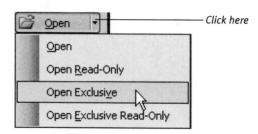

Figure 18.9 To remove a password, you must open the file in exclusive mode.

Figure 18.10 You must demonstrate that you know the password before you'll be allowed to remove it.

✔ Tips

- When creating your password, don't be obvious. Your name (as well as that of your child or pet), birthday, address, and phone number *are* obvious. A combination of letters and numbers is better.

- Don't mix letter case. *LizaRd289* will be difficult to remember and cumbersome to type. You'll find it easier if you use lower-case for all characters.

- Don't reuse passwords. Don't use your Internet account password for a database, for example.

PASSWORD-PROTECTING A DATABASE

Setting User-Level Security

The Workgroup Information File (WIF) is the repository of user-level security information. Once created, it contains the groups, users and passwords, and the specific permissions each user or group has been granted for a given database. Since you may want to set user-level security for multiple databases, you can have one WIF store the information for all of them or create several WIFs that you can switch among as needed.

Although you can create or modify a workgroup by using the tools in the Tools > Security submenu, the easiest way to initially set user-level security is by using the wizard provided for that purpose, as described in the next section.

✔ Tip

■ Adding user-level security is fraught with potential problems. For example, if you've already used the default WIF (created when Access is installed), there's no way to restore it without reinstalling Access. And the procedure to *remove* user-level security (in case you later change your mind) requires you to import all objects from the protected database into a new, blank database.

Thus, before creating a new workgroup, you're advised to make a backup copy of the default WIF. When adding user-level security to databases and creating additional WIFs, you should back up the unprotected databases, as well as the new WIFs. (WIF files have a .mdw extension.)

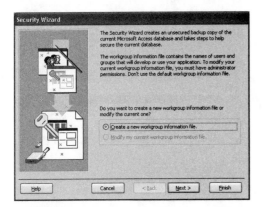

Figure 18.11 In the wizard's opening screen, indicate whether you want to create a new WIF or modify the current WIF (if you've previously created one).

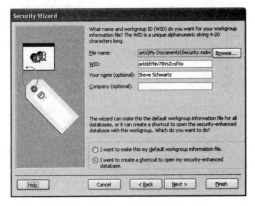

Figure 18.12 Name the new WIF, enter identifying information, and indicate whether this will be the default WIF.

The User-Level Security Wizard

You can use the User-Level Security Wizard to create the initial and subsequent WIFs or to modify an existing WIF. The steps below show you how to accomplish the following:

◆ If this is the first database you want to protect and you haven't previously created a WIF (and, hence, are still using the default WIF provided by Access), you will use the wizard to help create a new workgroup information file.

◆ If you've previously protected one or more databases and/or have already created a new WIF, you will use the wizard to modify the existing WIF by adding information for the new database.

To use the User-Level Security Wizard to create a new WIF:

1. As the administrator, open the database to which you want to add user-level security.

2. Choose Tools > Security > User-Level Security Wizard.
   The Security Wizard appears (**Figure 18.11**).

3. Select Create a new workgroup information file. Click Next.

4. In the new screen (**Figure 18.12**), do the following and then click Next.

   ▲ Accept the default WIF filename and location, or click Browse to specify a different one.

   ▲ Accept the proposed *WID* (Access' internal identification ID), or replace it with one of your own.

   ▲ *Optional:* Enter an identifying name and company.

   ▲ Click a radio button to make this the default WIF (to be used by all databases on this computer) or create a clickable shortcut to the current database.

   continues on next page

SETTING USER-LEVEL SECURITY

5. In the new screen (**Figure 18.13**), specify the database objects to be protected. Click tabs to view the various object classes. When you're done, click Next.

To avoid changing the security for previously protected objects, you can remove those checkmarks.

6. In the new screen (**Figure 18.14**), check the preset security groups that you'd like to include in the WIF. Each group has default permissions that appear when you highlight the group name. Click Next.

In addition to these basic groups, you can later create your own groups based on any criteria you want, such as employees of a particular department.

7. In the new screen (**Figure 18.15**), click a radio button to assign permissions to the Users group or to create the Users group without any permissions.

To assign permissions, click the tabs and check the appropriate boxes. When you're done, click Next.

8. In the new screen (**Figure 18.16**), you can add users. Enter the user's name, an initial password (it can be changed later), and then click Add This User to the List. When you're done, click Next.

9. In the new screen (**Figure 18.17**), assign each user to one or more groups. When you're done, click Next.

The permissions granted to each preset group are shown in **Table 18.1**.

10. Access assigns the selected security options to the current database and creates a backup copy of the unsecured database. To change the name or location of the backup, edit the file path in the text box or click Browse. Click Finish to proceed.

11. Access creates a report that you can print for a permanent record. You can also save the report as a Snapshot (.snp) file.

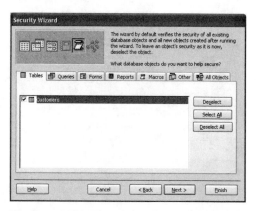

Figure 18.13 Click tabs and check the objects to protect.

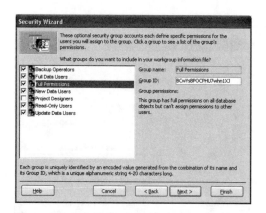

Figure 18.14 Specify the default groups to establish.

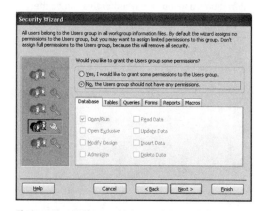

Figure 18.15 Indicate which permissions—if any—will be granted to the default Users group.

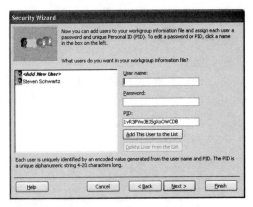

Figure 18.16 Add users to the workgroup.

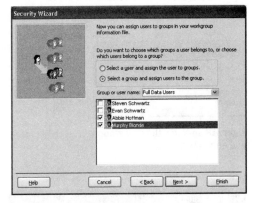

Figure 18.17 Assign users to groups.

Table 18.1

Permissions for the Preset Groups	
GROUP	PERMISSIONS
Backup Operators	Backup and compact database only
Full Data Users	Edit data, but not modify objects
Full Permissions	Add or modify objects
New Data Users	Read and add data only
Project Designers	Edit data and modify objects, but not modify tables or relationships
Read-Only Users	Read data only
Update Data Users	Read and update data, but not add new records or delete data

To use the User-Level Security Wizard to modify the current WIF:

1. As the administrator, open a previously secured database or another database that you now want to secure.

2. Choose Tools > Security > User-Level Security Wizard.

   The Security Wizard appears (see Figure 18.11).

3. Select Modify my current workgroup information file. Click Next.

4. Follow Steps 5–10 from the previous list.

   You can enable additional default groups, change permissions for the Users group, add more users, and/or alter the membership of the current groups.

✔ Tips

■ The administrator can also create a new workgroup by doing little more than naming it. Choose Tools > Security > Workgroup Administrator, and click the Create button.

■ Although you can create as many WIFs as you like (one for each database, for example), whenever you attempt to open a database, you will have to "join" the appropriate WIF (as explained later in this chapter). For this reason, you may find it preferable to simply modify the current WIF for each new database that you want to protect.

■ If you save the report as a Snapshot file, you will probably want to move or save it to a removable disk (such as a floppy). Snapshot files are *not* secure, so leaving the file on your hard disk creates a security risk.

■ Setting user-level security can also be useful if you're developing databases that you intend to sell or distribute as shareware. For example, you could create several groups with progressively greater permissions, and sell the database at different prices, depending on the permissions granted.

SETTING USER-LEVEL SECURITY

Creating additional groups

The User-Level Security Wizard helps create several generic groups, based strictly on the general permissions that each has. While this will often suffice, there will also be occasions when you'll want to create your own groups. For instance, you may need to assign permissions according to a user's department, such as Accounting or Administration. Or you may want to prevent certain objects from even being viewed by some groups.

The first step is to create the new groups. Then you can set general permissions for the groups, as well as permissions for specific objects. (Note that the User and Group Accounts command is also used to *delete* groups, as well as to add or delete users.)

To create or delete groups:

1. Launch Access, open the database, log on as the administrator, and choose Tools > Security > User and Group Accounts.

    The User and Group Accounts dialog box appears.

2. Click the Groups tab (**Figure 18.18**).

3. *Do one of the following:*

    ▲ To create a new group, click the New button. In the New User/Group dialog box (**Figure 18.19**), name the group, enter an ID containing between 4 and 20 characters, and click OK.

    ▲ To delete an existing group, select its name from the Name drop-down list, click Delete, and then click Yes in the confirmation dialog box that appears.

4. To assign users to a new group, click the Users tab (**Figure 18.20**). From the Name drop-down list, select a user you'd like to assign to the new group, select the group name from the Available Groups list, and click the Add button.

5. When you're done, click OK.

Figure 18.18 Click New to create a new group.

Figure 18.19 Name the new group and enter an ID for it.

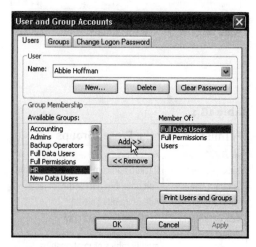

Figure 18.20 To add a user as a new group member, select his/her name, select the group name, and click Add.

Figure 18.21 Use this dialog box to set basic and object level permissions for any user or group.

Setting permissions for specific objects

The User-Level Security Group Permissions Wizard can set permissions for *classes* of objects (such as all tables), but not *specific* objects (such as a particular table). To restrict access to an object or to limit the activities a user or group can perform on an object, you use the User and Group Permissions command.

To set specific object permissions for users or groups:

1. As the administrator, open the database and choose Tools > Security > User and Group Permissions.

   The User and Group Permissions dialog box appears (**Figure 18.21**).

2. On the Permissions tab of the dialog box, click either the Users or the Groups radio button (depending on which permissions you want to review or change).

3. Select a user or group name, an object type, and the specific object (or objects) for which you want to set permissions.

   You can also select <New *object type*> to set the same permissions for all new objects of the chosen type, such as forms.

4. Enter a checkmark for each permission that you want the user or group to have for the selected object, and then click Apply.

5. Repeat Steps 3 and 4 as necessary.

6. Click OK to close the dialog box.

Switching workgroups

If you've secured different databases in different workgroups, it will be necessary to *join* the correct workgroup before you will be allowed to open a given database.

To switch workgroups:

1. Choose Tools > Security > Workgroup Administrator.

The Workgroup Administrator dialog box appears (**Figure 18.22**).

2. Click the Join button.

The Workgroup Information File dialog box appears (**Figure 18.23**).

3. Type the path to or browse for the desired workgroup, and then click OK.

You'll now be allowed to open the database.

Figure 18.22 Use the Workgroup Administrator dialog box to switch from one workgroup to another.

Type the WIF path...   *...or browse for the file*

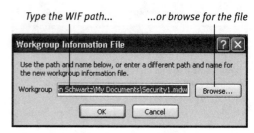

Figure 18.23 Specify the name and location of the workgroup file to which you want to switch.

Figure 18.24 Log on, entering the current password (if there is one).

Figure 18.25 To change passwords, enter the old and the new password. (If there is no current password, leave the Old Password text box blank.)

Changing passwords

When a database is first secured, passwords for the administrator and all new users are either blank or temporary ones assigned by the administrator. A user may set or change his or her password by following the steps below.

To change a user password:

1. Launch Access and immediately switch to the workgroup that contains the password you want to change. (See "Switching workgroups" on the previous page.)

2. Open a database that's secured by the current workgroup. Log on by entering your user name and password in the Logon dialog box (**Figure 18.24**).

3. Choose Tools > Security > User and Group Accounts.

   The User and Group Accounts dialog box appears (**Figure 18.25**).

4. Click the Change Logon Password tab.

5. In the text boxes provided, enter the old password, the new password (in both the New Password and the Verify text boxes), and then click Apply.

6. Click OK to dismiss the dialog box.

✔ Tip

- The database administrator can change a user's password by logging in as the user and following these steps.

SETTING USER-LEVEL SECURITY

19

AUTOMATING ACCESS

You can accomplish almost anything you want to do in Access by opening objects in the Database window, choosing menu commands, clicking icons, and painstakingly creating and applying filters. However, performing actions manually is often the hard way—and unnecessarily hard at that.

In this chapter, you'll learn how to automate actions by doing the following:

◆ Create a switchboard that serves as an interface for your database.

◆ Create command buttons for forms and data access pages that perform an action when clicked.

◆ Design macros that can perform single- or multistep actions.

Creating Switchboards

When you open the Northwind sample database, it displays a splash screen followed by an unusual dialog box with buttons for performing common tasks. This dialog box (**Figure 19.1**) is known as a *switchboard*. You can create one (or several) for any of your own databases.

To create a switchboard:

1. Open the database for which you want to create a switchboard.

2. Choose Tools > Database Utilities > Switchboard Manager.

   If a switchboard doesn't already exist for the database, a dialog box appears, asking if you'd like to create a switchboard.

3. Click Yes to create the initial switchboard. The Switchboard Manager appears (**Figure 19.2**).

4. Select the switchboard and click Edit.

   The Edit Switchboard Page dialog box appears, ready to receive new items.

5. *Optional:* You can rename the switchboard by typing in the Switchboard Name text box. The Switchboard Name will appear in the Title area of the switchboard's dialog box.

6. To add an item to the switchboard, click New. The Edit Switchboard Item dialog box appears.

7. Create the new item (**Figure 19.3**) by doing the following:

   ▲ In the Text box, enter the text that will label this item's button.

   ▲ From the Command drop-down list, select the command that you want the button to perform.

   ▲ Select an item from the bottom drop-down list. (The listed items vary, depending on the command selected.)

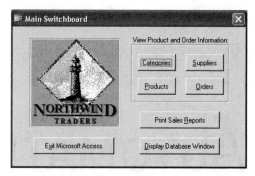

Figure 19.1 The Northwind database presents this switchboard, enabling users to perform functions by clicking buttons.

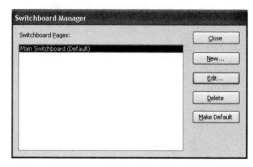

Figure 19.2 The Switchboard Manager lists switchboards that have been created for the database.

Figure 19.3 To create a new item, name it, select a command to perform, and then specify the database object that the command will affect.

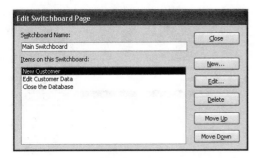

Figure 19.4 The Edit Switchboard Page lists all items that have been defined for the current switchboard.

Title   Buttons

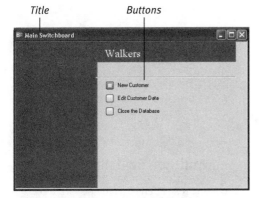

Figure 19.5 This is the general layout of a switchboard created with the Switchboard Manager.

Select a switchboard

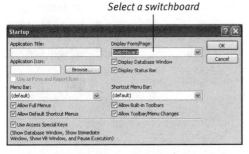

Figure 19.6 You can specify that a switchboard will automatically appear when you open the database.

8. Click OK.
   The new item is added to the switchboard.

9. As needed, repeat Steps 6–8 to add other items to the switchboard (**Figure 19.4**).

10. When you're done, click Close to dismiss the Edit Switchboard Page. Click close again to close the Switchboard Manager.

11. To view the switchboard (**Figure 19.5**), double-click its entry in the Forms section of the Database window.

✔ Tips

■ The following are the simplest commands to include in a switchboard:

▲ **Go to Switchboard.** Replace the switchboard button list with buttons from another designated switchboard.

▲ **Open Form in Add Mode.** Create a new record using the specified form.

▲ **Open Form in Edit Mode.** View, edit, or add records using the specified form.

▲ **Open Report.** Open the specified report in preview mode.

▲ **Exit Application.** Close the current database.

■ Only switchboards created with the Switchboard Manager can be edited with the Switchboard Manager. Others (such as those generated by creating a new database using a wizard) aren't listed in the Switchboard Manager dialog box.

■ Switchboard Manager switchboards are presentable, but could use some dressing up. For instructions on making some simple design modifications to a switchboard, see the next section.

■ To automatically display a switchboard whenever you open the database, choose Tools > Startup. In the Startup dialog box (**Figure 19.6**), select the switchboard's name from the Display Form/Page drop-down list and click OK.

CREATING SWITCHBOARDS

Modifying Switchboards

A switchboard created with the Switchboard Manager can be modified and embellished in two ways: by using the Switchboard Manager or by switching to Design View. Use the Switchboard Manager to edit, add, delete, or change the order of items. Use Design View to add an image (such as a logo) to your switchboard or to make other manual design changes.

To modify a switchboard using the Switchboard Manager:

1. Open the database whose switchboard you want to change.

2. Choose Tools > Database Utilities > Switchboard Manager.

   The Switchboard Manager appears (see Figure 19.2).

3. Select the switchboard that you want to modify, and then click Edit.

   The Edit Switchboard Page appears (**Figure 19.7**).

4. *Do any of the following:*
   ▲ To change the order in which items are presented, select an item and click Move Up or Move Down.
   ▲ Click Edit to modify a selected item—changing its text or what it does.
   ▲ Click Delete to remove a selected item.
   ▲ Click New to add another item.

5. When you're done, click Close to dismiss each of the dialog boxes.

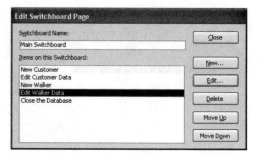

Figure 19.7 All editing commands (other than creating a new item) require that you first select an item from the list.

Multiple Switchboards

You aren't restricted to a single switchboard per database (although one will frequently suffice). For instance, if a database has many forms and reports, you can create additional switchboards to present the lists of forms and reports. The default switchboard might present only general options, such as Data Entry, Choose Forms, and Choose Reports. When one of the latter buttons is clicked, the appropriate subordinate switchboard button list replaces the main list.

To accomplish the switch between switchboards, assign the Go to Switchboard command to each of the latter buttons and specify the particular switchboard to display. To enable the user to revert to the main switchboard, include a Go to Switchboard button in each of the subordinate switchboards. When they're clicked, the main switchboard appears.

Browse images

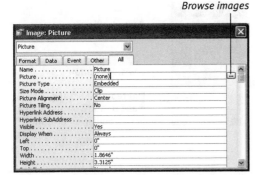

Figure 19.8 You can insert a picture into a switchboard and set basic formatting options for it.

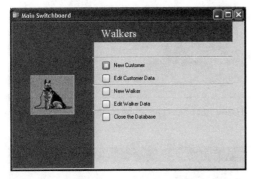

Figure 19.9 This modified switchboard includes a picture and additional horizontal rules which split the commands into logical groups.

To modify a switchboard in Design View:

1. Open the database whose switchboard you want to change.

2. Double-click the switchboard in the Forms section of the Database window. The Switchboard opens.

3. Switch to Design View by clicking the View toolbar icon or by choosing View > Design View.

4. To add an image or logo to the switchboard, do the following:

   ▲ Select the picture area (the green section on the left side of the switchboard).

   ▲ Click the Properties toolbar icon, choose View > Properties, or press Alt Enter. The Image: Picture dialog box appears (**Figure 19.8**).

   ▲ On the All tab, click in the Picture item. Click the browse button that appears and select an image. The image is added to the switchboard.

   ▲ Select a sizing option from the drop-down list in the Size Mode item: Clip, Stretch, or Zoom. The image automatically adjusts to the selected setting.

   ▲ Select an alignment setting for the picture from the Picture Alignment drop-down list.

   ▲ Close the Image: Picture dialog box.

5. Make any other desired changes, such as altering the title text, adding additional horizontal rules, or adding other embellishments.

6. Switch to Form View (**Figure 19.9**) to examine your changes. (Click the View toolbar icon or choose View > Form View.)

✔ Tip

■ Rather than relying on Size Mode, you may have better luck just resizing the picture as needed in an image-editing program.

MODIFYING SWITCHBOARDS

Creating Command Buttons

Command buttons are similar to switchboard buttons. However, command buttons are placed on a form or data access page. When the user clicks a command button, the single action associated with the button is performed, such as opening another form, applying a filter, or printing the current record. The simplest way to create a command button is to use the Command Button Wizard.

To create a command button:

1. Open a form or data access page in Design View.

2. Click the Command Button icon in the Toolbox (**Figure 19.10**). Be sure that the Control Wizards icon is enabled.

3. Drag a button outline to the desired spot on the form or data access page.

   The Command Button Wizard opens (**Figure 19.11**).

4. Select a command button category and the specific action that you want the button to perform. Click Next to continue.

   For some actions, you may also have to specify a target object and/or other options.

5. Specify a button label (**Figure 19.12**) by doing one of the following:

   ▲ To display a text label on the button, click the Text radio button, accept or edit the text, and click Next.

   ▲ To display a picture on the button, click the Picture radio button, select an image from the list (or click Browse to use an image stored on disk), and click Next.

6. On the final screen, name the button and click Finish to return to Design View.

7. *Optional:* Click and drag to change the button's size or placement.

8. Switch to Form View (**Figure 19.13**) and test the button.

CREATING COMMAND BUTTONS

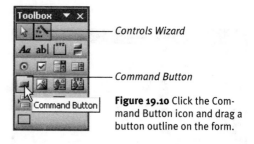

Controls Wizard

Command Button

Figure 19.10 Click the Command Button icon and drag a button outline on the form.

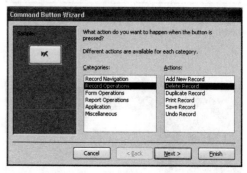

Figure 19.11 Select an action for the button to perform.

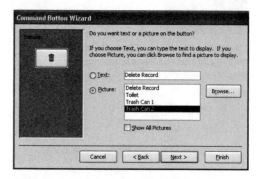

Figure 19.12 Specify a text or picture label.

Figure 19.13 Test the finished button in Form View.

About Macros

Unlike switchboard items and command buttons, macros can execute a complex series of actions. For example, a macro could open a form, select a record subset, sort the records in a particular order, print, resort the records, and then close the form. A macro step can even use a conditional test to determine which of two sets of actions to take.

Any macro can be executed from the Database window or by choosing the Tools > Macro > Run Macro command. You can also attach a macro to a command button, enabling it to be executed with a click.

The following pages explain the basics of creating, running, and editing macros. When you start making your own macros, you will want to consult—and possibly print out—the Help sections on macro actions and their arguments. (Open the Access Help Table of Contents and expand the section entitled *Programmability: Actions.*)

Attaching Macros to Objects

Associating a macro with a command button is only one of many options you have when it comes to specifying conditions that will trigger a macro's execution. For example, you can cause a macro to run whenever a particular field is entered or exited. Entering the field could run a macro to display data entry help text, for instance.

To link a macro to a field or other object on a form, open the form in Design View, right-click the object (such as a field or graphic), and choose Properties. Click the Event tab on the dialog box that appears. Click in the trigger event that you want to use (such as On Exit or On Click), and select the macro's name from the drop-down list.

Creating Macros

Creating a macro is similar to programming. Rather than hand-typing code as you do in most development environments, you create macros by selecting actions and arguments from drop-down lists.

To create a macro:

1. Display the Database window, click the Macros object, and then click the New icon at the top of the Database window.

   An empty Macro window appears (**Figure 19.14**). The insertion mark is positioned in the first cell of the Action column.

2. Click the arrow at the right side of the Action column and select the macro's first action from the drop-down list (**Figure 19.15**).

3. Most macro actions require one or more arguments. Specify arguments at the bottom of the window (**Figure 19.16**).

   The type and number of arguments, as well as how they're specified, vary according to the action. Many action arguments can be selected from drop-down lists, while others must be typed or pasted into a text box.

4. *Optional:* Add an explanatory comment in the Comments column to document the macro action.

5. Repeat Steps 2–4 for each additional action.

6. *Optional:* Actions are performed sequentially, starting from the top. To change the order of any action, select its indicator and then drag it up or down in the list.

7. When you're done, click the window's close box. Click Yes when prompted to save the macro.

   A Save As dialog box appears (**Figure 19.17**).

8. Enter a name for the macro and click OK.

   The macro is added as a new object to the Macros section of the Database window.

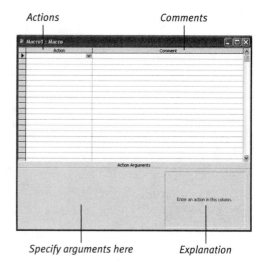

Actions   *Comments*

Specify arguments here   *Explanation*

Figure 19.14 A new macro window.

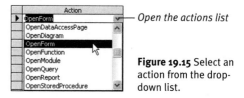

Open the actions list

Figure 19.15 Select an action from the drop-down list.

Figure 19.16 Specify arguments for the current action. (Available arguments depend on the action type.)

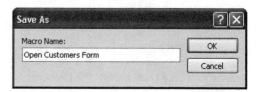

Figure 19.17 Name the new macro and then click OK.

Macro Name column ┌─ Macro Names icon

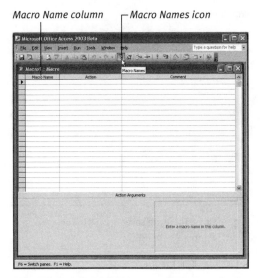

Figure 19.18 To create a macro group, you need to add the Macro Name column to the window.

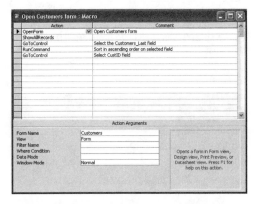

Figure 19.19 The Open Customers Form macro.

✔ Tips

- If the argument for an action is a database object, you can drag the object into the Object Name box rather than typing or pasting the object's name.

- When creating a command button with the Command Button Wizard, you can attach a macro to the button by selecting the Miscellaneous category and the Run Macro action. Select the macro to use from the list presented in the next dialog box.

- If a database will require many macros, you can group related ones together to form a *macro group*. Start as though creating a single macro. When the Macro window opens, click the Macro Names toolbar icon. A Macro Name column is added at the left side of the window (**Figure 19.18**).

  Create the macros as usual, but name each one as you would otherwise have done in the Save As dialog box. To start each new macro, begin on a new line—being sure to specify a new Macro Name. The Macro Name column should be blank for all other lines of the macro. After you save a macro group, individual macros within the group are referenced using the group name, a period (.), and the specific macro name, such as *forms.customers*.

- **Table 19.1** explains the steps of a simple macro that was created to open a form, sorted on a selected field (**Figure 19.19**).

CREATING MACROS

Table 19.1

A Macro Example		
ACTION	**ARGUMENTS**	**EXPLANATION**
OpenForm	Form Name: Customers; View: Form	Open the Customers form
ShowAllRecords	[none]	Remove any applied filters, showing all records
GoToControl	Control Name: Customers_Last	Select the last name field (Customers_Last)
RunCommand	Command: SortAscending	Perform an ascending sort on the Customers_Last field
GoToControl	Control Name: CustID	Select the CustID field, making it the current focus

Running Macros

Creating a functioning macro is much more than an exercise in programming proficiency. A macro is useful only if it can be conveniently executed. The following list shows the most common methods of running a macro.

To run a macro:

◆ Double-click the macro in the Database window.

◆ Select the macro in the Database window, and click the Run toolbar icon (**Figure 19.20**).

◆ Right-click the macro in the Database window, and choose Run from the pop-up menu that appears.

◆ Choose Tools > Macro > Run Macro. Select the macro from the drop-down list in the Run Macro dialog box (**Figure 19.21**), and then click OK.

◆ Perform the action (if any) that you've associated with the macro, such as clicking a command button.

◆ When creating or editing a macro in Design View, click the Run toolbar icon or choose Run > Run.

✔ Tip

■ If a macro doesn't perform as expected, you can run it in single-step mode and see what happens at each step. Open the macro in Design View, and choose Run > Single Step or click the Single Step toolbar icon. Then run the macro by choosing Run > Run or by clicking the Run toolbar icon.

Examine the information presented in the Macro Single Step dialog box (**Figure 19.22**) and click Step to execute the next macro line. As you step through the macro, the action for each line is performed.

Run toolbar icon

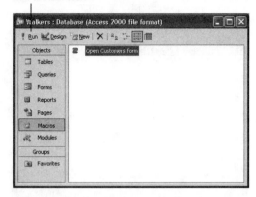

Figure 19.20 There are several ways to run a macro from the Database window.

Figure 19.21 Select the macro name from the drop-down list and click OK to run it.

Figure 19.22 You can single step through a macro to see if each action performs correctly. Click Continue to exit step mode and complete the remaining steps. To immediately stop the execution, click Halt.

RUNNING MACROS

Editing Macros

A macro is a program—generally, a *small* program, but a program nonetheless. As such, it may not always perform as you expect. Or perhaps you've decided that some of its actions are unnecessary or that additional ones need to be added. You can freely edit a macro, as explained in the following step list.

To edit a macro:

1. Select the macro in the Database window, and click the Design toolbar icon.

   The Macro window opens (**Figure 19.23**).

2. *Do any of the following:*

   ▲ Press Del to remove a selected action.

   ▲ To move an action to a new position in the list, click its selector and drag the action up or down.

   ▲ To insert an action, click a selector and choose Insert > Rows (or click the Insert Rows toolbar icon). A blank row will appear above the selected action.

   ▲ To edit an action or its comment or arguments, click to select the appropriate part of the action and use normal editing techniques, such as retyping and selecting from drop-down lists.

   ▲ To specify a conditional test for an action, click the Conditions toolbar icon. A Condition column appears in which you can type or paste a conditional expression.

3. Close the Macro window and save the changes when prompted to do so.

✔ Tips

■ To rename a macro, right-click it in the Database window and choose Rename from the pop-up menu (**Figure 19.24**).

■ To delete a macro, select it in the Database window, and click the Delete toolbar icon or press Del.

Figure 19.23 Most modifications to a macro are done in Design View in a Macro window.

Figure 19.24 Right-click a macro in the Database window to reveal many useful commands, such as Rename, Delete, Run, and Design View.

EDITING MACROS

20

CUSTOMIZING ACCESS

Access provides many ways for you to customize your user experience, making it more comfortable, convenient, and expedient.

In this chapter, you'll learn how to make the following customizations:

◆ Modifying the standard menus and toolbars by moving, adding, and deleting commands and elements

◆ Creating custom toolbars and menus

◆ Setting toolbar and menu preferences

◆ Setting program preferences in the Options dialog box

Customizing Toolbars

As good as they are, you aren't stuck with Access' standard toolbars. You can rearrange, remove, or add elements freely in order to make them fit your work style. Unlike creating a custom toolbar (which affects only the database that was open when the toolbar was created), changes made to standard toolbars are global.

Note that when modifying toolbars, you can copy or move elements within the same toolbar or between toolbars.

To move, copy, or add toolbar elements:

1. Choose Tools > Customize.

   The Customize dialog box appears.

2. Click the Toolbars tab (**Figure 20.1**).

3. Display the toolbars that you want to change by clicking their checkboxes.

4. *Do one of the following:*

   ▲ To *move* a toolbar icon or menu from one location to another, click the element and then drag it into position on the target toolbar.

   ▲ To *copy* a toolbar icon or menu from one location to another, Ctrl-click the element and then drag it into position on the target toolbar.

   ▲ To *add* a new element to a toolbar, click the Commands tab (**Figure 20.2**), select a category, select the desired command, and drag it into position on the target toolbar.

   The selected element is surrounded by a black box. The target position of the element is indicated by an I-beam cursor (**Figure 20.3**). Release the mouse button to complete the move, copy, or addition.

5. Make any other desired changes and close the Customize dialog box.

Figure 20.1 Check toolbar names in order to display and modify them.

Category list   *Command list*

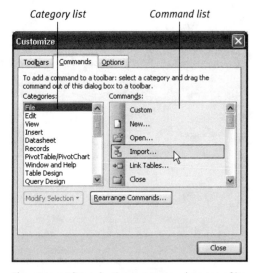

Figure 20.2 After selecting a category, drag one of its commands onto a displayed toolbar.

I-beam

Figure 20.3 The I-beam cursor shows where the moved or copied element will be placed when you release the mouse button.

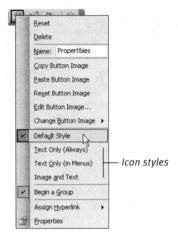

 —— Icon styles

Default Style

Text Only

Image and Text

Figure 20.4 Right-click a toolbar icon and choose a style (top) to apply to the icon (bottom).

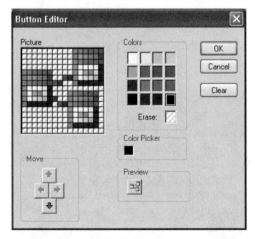

Figure 20.5 You can use the Button Editor to customize the appearance of a toolbar icon.

✔ Tips

- To remove a toolbar element, right-click it and choose Delete from the pop-up menu.

- To restore a modified toolbar to its state when Access was installed, highlight it in the Customize dialog box and click Reset (see Figure 20.1).

- To change the style of a single toolbar icon, right-click it and choose Default Style, Text Only, or Image and Text (**Figure 20.4**).

- To change a toolbar icon's image, you can do any of the following:
  - ▲ Right-click the icon and choose a new image from the Change Button Image submenu.
  - ▲ If you've copied a graphic to the Clipboard, you can use it as the new icon by choosing Paste Button Image.
  - ▲ If you're feeling artistic (and adventurous), you can modify an icon using the Button Editor (**Figure 20.5**). To open the Button Editor, right-click the icon and choose Edit Button Image.

- You can also display the right-click pop-up menu for a selected element by clicking the Modify Selection button (found on the Commands tab of the Customize dialog box).

- If you later change your mind and want to restore the original/default icon, right-click the icon and choose Reset Button Image.

- Rather than make extensive modifications to the standard toolbars, you may find it more convenient to create custom-purpose toolbars of your own. The Utility 1 and Utility 2 toolbars are provided for this purpose. Both are initially blank and ready to receive new elements.

CUSTOMIZING TOOLBARS

Creating New Toolbars

In addition to modifying the standard toolbars, you can create a custom toolbar from scratch. A custom toolbar is only displayed in and available to the database with which it's associated. To reuse a custom toolbar in a different database, you must either re-create or import it.

To create a custom toolbar:

1. Open the database with which the custom toolbar will be associated.

2. Choose Tools > Customize.
   The Customize dialog box appears.

3. On the Toolbars tab (see Figure 20.1), click the New button.
   The New Toolbar dialog box appears (**Figure 20.6**).

4. Enter a name for the new toolbar and click OK.
   An empty toolbar appears (**Figure 20.7**). The new toolbar's name is added to the bottom of the list in the Customize dialog box.

5. Drag elements to the toolbar as described in the previous step list. Then close the Customize dialog box.

✔ Tip

■ You can modify a user-created toolbar (renaming, deleting, changing the icons, and so on) by following the instructions and tips in the previous step list.

Figure 20.6 Name the new toolbar and click OK.

Figure 20.7 Drag elements onto this tiny, empty toolbar.

Auto-Adjusting Toolbars and Menus

By default, Access and other Office applications continually monitor which menu commands and toolbar elements you use—and adjust themselves accordingly. Seldom-used items are hidden or removed; items that you regularly use are moved to more prominent positions. Thus, some of the manual changes to toolbars or menus that you might want to make may conceivably be made for you—*automatically!*

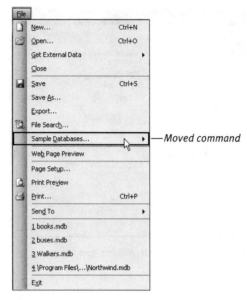

Figure 20.8 To make it easier to find the sample databases, I moved them to the File menu.

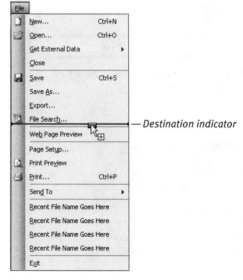

Figure 20.9 A command's destination is indicated by a horizontal bar.

Customizing Menus

Like toolbars, built-in menus can be customized by adding, removing, moving, or renaming commands. For example, if a command is hard for you to find, you can move it to a new spot in the current menu or a different menu.

To customize the standard menus:

1. Choose Tools > Customize.

   The Customize dialog box appears.

2. *Do one of the following:*

   ▲ To *move* a command from one menu location to another, open the original menu, select the command, and then drag it into its new position.

   If the target is a different menu, drag onto the menu title (such as File). The menu will drop down, enabling you to select a destination (**Figure 20.8**).

   ▲ To *copy* a command from one location to another, Ctrl-click the command and then drag it into position.

   ▲ To *add* a new command to a menu, click the Commands tab (see Figure 20.2), select a category, select a command, and drag it into position on the target menu.

   A selected menu title or command is surrounded by a black box. The target of the command is indicated by a horizontal bar (**Figure 20.9**). Release the mouse button to complete the move, copy, or addition.

3. Make any other desired changes and close the Customize dialog box.

✔ Tips

■ When selecting a command to move/copy, if you open the wrong menu, click it again to close it or click a different menu.

■ To reset the menus, select Menu Bar on the Toolbars tab, and then click Reset.

Creating a Custom Menu

You can also add a custom menu with its own commands that will be nestled among Access' standard menus. The menu title will always be visible—regardless of the database that was active when the menu was created. The menu contents, on the other hand, are database specific; that is, the menu will only display commands when the database with which it's associated is active.

To add a custom menu:

1. Open the database with which the custom menu will be associated.

2. Choose Tools > Customize.
   The Customize dialog box appears.

3. On the Commands tab, select New Menu from the Categories list (**Figure 20.10**).

4. Drag the New Menu command into the desired spot on the menu bar and release the mouse button.

5. Right-click the New Menu menu title. In the pop-up menu that appears (**Figure 20.11**), enter a new name for the menu title in the Name text box, and then press Enter.

6. Drag commands to the menu using the methods described in the prior step lists.

7. When you've finished constructing the menu, close the Customize dialog box.

✔ Tip

■ Can't come up with a reason to create custom menus? Think how handy it would be if you could open your forms, reports, or queries from a menu. To add such items to a menu, choose All Forms, All Reports, or All Queries from the Categories list and then drag any of your listed forms, reports, or queries into the new menu (**Figure 20.12**).

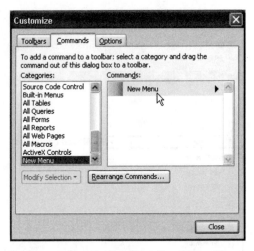

Figure 20.10 Drag the New Menu item into position in the menu bar.

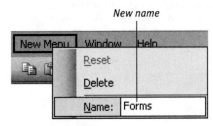

Figure 20.11 Right-click the New Menu item and then rename it.

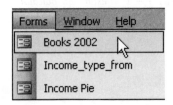

Figure 20.12 The new Forms menu provides access to the database's forms.

Figure 20.13 Set menu and toolbar preferences on the Options tab of the Customize dialog box.

Figure 20.14 The Expand indicator appears at the bottom of abbreviated Office menus.

Toolbar and Menu Preferences

You can customize the display and the manner in which toolbars and menus operate by changing settings on the Options tab of the Customize dialog box. Note that these settings affect *all* Office programs, not just Access.

To set toolbar and menu preferences:

1. Choose Tools > Customize.

   The Customize dialog box appears.

2. Click the Options tab (**Figure 20.13**).

3. You can set any of the following options:

   ▲ **Always show full menus.** When checked, Office's abbreviated, auto-expanding menus are replaced by full menus. When unchecked, abbreviated menus with an Expand indicator at the bottom are presented (**Figure 20.14**).

   ▲ **Show full menus after a short delay.** This option is available only when Always show full menus isn't checked. When this option is selected, menus automatically expand when the cursor rests for a moment over an expand indicator. If the box is unchecked, menus expand only when you click the Expand indicator.

   ▲ **Reset menu and toolbar usage data.** Access tracks the menu commands and toolbar elements that you use. The data is used to adjust the menus and toolbars. If the data seems to be erroneous or the primary Access user on the computer has changed, you can click this button to reset the tracking data.

   ▲ **Large icons.** Replaces the toolbar icons with oversized ones.

   continues on next page

▲ **List font names in their font.** To make it easy to choose the correct font, you can display each font name in its own font. (If you have a large number of fonts, this can slow the display of the font list.)

▲ **Show ScreenTips on toolbars.** When checked, if you rest the cursor over a toolbar element for a moment, the element's name appears (**Figure 20.15**).

▲ **Show shortcut keys in ScreenTips.** When checked, a toolbar element's shortcut key (if it has one) is displayed as part of the ScreenTip (**Figure 20.16**).

▲ **Menu animations.** Select a technique used to animate submenus as they open (**Figure 20.17**).

Figure 20.15 An example of a ScreenTip.

Figure 20.16 ScreenTips can also be set to show shortcut keys.

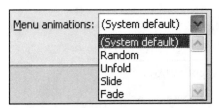

Figure 20.17 You can choose any of these menu animation techniques. (Random draws from all of the techniques.)

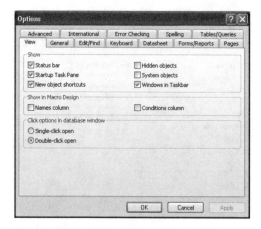

Figure 20.18 The View tab of the Options dialog box.

Program Preferences

In the Options dialog box, you can set many program defaults and preferences (referred to as *options*). Some apply only to the database that's open when they're set, while others are always in effect (regardless of what database is in use). The most important options are discussed in the pages that follow. (Options from the Pages and Error Checking tabs are not discussed.)

To set new options:

1. Open a database.

   Options can only be set if a database is open.

2. Choose Tools > Options.

   The Options dialog box appears, open to the most recently used tab (**Figure 20.18**).

3. Make any desired changes, switching to other tabs as necessary. Click Apply.

4. When you're through, click OK to close the Options dialog box.

View options

The View options (see Figure 20.18) enable you to show or hide interface elements and program components.

- ◆ **Show.** Determines whether components are shown or hidden.

   Depending on your work style, you may want to disable Startup Task Pane and New object shortcuts. If you generally work only with existing databases, having to dismiss the Startup Task Pane can be annoying. Hiding the New object shortcuts (such as Create table by using wizard) will result in only forms, queries, and so on being shown in the Database window.

- ◆ **Click options in database window.** This setting determines whether you must single- or double-click an object in the Database window to open or activate it.

✔ Tip

- ■ To view a brief explanation of any item in the Options dialog box, click the Help question mark (?) in the upper-right corner (see Figure 20.18) and then click the item for which you need help.

General options

The General tab (**Figure 20.19**) lists a variety of settings. It's a catchall category.

◆ **Print margins.** Specify the default margin settings for printouts.

◆ **Use four-digit year formatting.** Set 4-digit years (2003, for example) as the default year format for this and/or all Access databases (depending on the checked box or boxes). Using 4-digit years avoids the century confusion that may arise if only two digits are used for the year formatting.

◆ **New database sort order.** If your databases are normally in some language other than English, select a language from this drop-down list.

◆ **Recently used file list.** To make it easier to reopen recently used databases, they can be listed at the bottom of the File menu (**Figure 20.20**). Select the number of recent databases to track from the drop-down list.

◆ **Compact on close.** Set this option to automatically compact and repair databases whenever they're closed.

◆ **Default database folder.** Enter the full DOS pathname for the directory in which you want to store most of your databases. When you create a new database, Access will automatically propose this folder as the one in which to save the file.

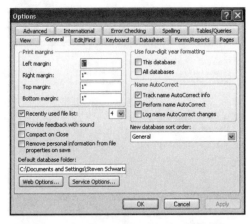

Figure 20.19 The General tab of the Options dialog box.

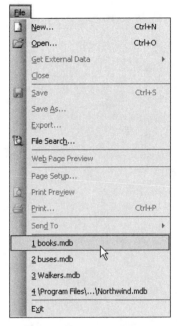

Figure 20.20 Recently opened databases can be listed and chosen from the bottom of the File menu.

PROGRAM PREFERENCES

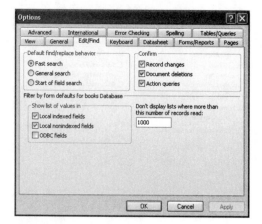

Figure 20.21 The Edit/Find tab of the Options dialog box.

Figure 20.22 Confirmation dialog boxes like this one are the default, but they aren't mandatory. (However, they do help many people.)

Edit/Find options

Use the Edit/Find tab (**Figure 20.21**) to set the default Find/Replace behavior and specify edit actions that require user conformation.

◆ **Default find/replace behavior.** This option specifies the settings to use when you open the Find and Replace dialog box. *Fast search* restricts the search to the current field and must match the entire field. *General search* searches all fields and can match any part of a field. *Start of field search* searches only the current field and must match the beginning of the field.

A change in this setting takes effect after you quit and restart Access.

◆ **Confirm.** By default, editing actions that result in irreversible changes to the database must be confirmed (**Figure 20.22**). If you feel that certain confirmation dialog boxes are no longer necessary, you can remove their checkmarks.

Keyboard options

Use the Keyboard tab (**Figure 20.23**) to specify the way that Access behaves when you're entering data and moving from field to field.

◆ **Move after enter.** Determines what happens when the insertion point is in a field and you press ⏎.

▲ *Don't move.* The insertion point stays in the current field.

▲ *Next field.* The insertion point moves to the next field of the current record.

▲ *Next record.* The insertion point moves to the same field in the next record.

◆ **Behavior entering field.** Determines what happens when you tab into a field.

▲ *Select entire field.* All characters in the field are selected, enabling you to overwrite or delete the data with a single keystroke.

▲ *Go to start of field.* The insertion point is positioned for editing at the start of the field.

▲ *Go to end of field.* The insertion point is positioned for editing at the end of the field.

◆ **Arrow key behavior.** Determines what happens when you press an arrow key.

▲ *Next field.* Left and right arrow keys behave like the Tab key. Unless you've clicked in a field to set the insertion point for editing, pressing an arrow key moves you from field to field.

▲ *Next character.* Pressing the left or right arrow key automatically puts you into edit mode for the current field. To move to the next field, you can press Tab or press → when the insertion point is to the right of the last character in a field.

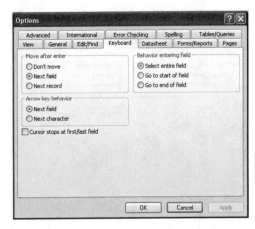

Figure 20.23 The Keyboard tab of the Options dialog box.

Figure 20.24 The Datasheet tab of the Options dialog box.

Datasheet options

You use the Datasheet tab (**Figure 20.24**) to specify default appearance settings for all datasheets.

The options are fairly self-explanatory. You can change the display colors of various elements, set the default font that is used to display data, specify whether or not gridlines are visible, and set a new default column width. The most dramatic change that you can make is to select a new Default cell effect (**Figure 20.25**).

✔ Tip

- Changes made to the Datasheet options affect all datasheets—both old and new— for all databases. To see the new effect(s), you must close and then reopen any datasheets that are currently open.

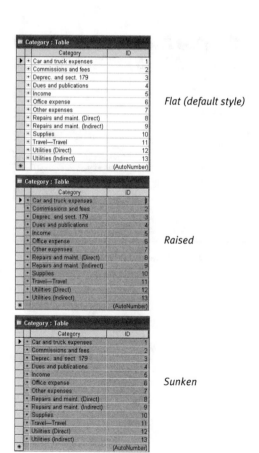

Flat (default style)

Raised

Sunken

Figure 20.25 Datasheet styles.

Forms/Reports options

The options on the Forms/Reports tab (**Figure 20.26**) enable you to set defaults for important form- and report-creation procedures.

- **Selection behavior.** Determines how objects are selected when you're designing a report or form. If you choose *Partially enclosed,* simply passing the selection rectangle through an object will select it. *Fully enclosed* requires an object to be completely surrounded by the selection rectangle in order to be selected.

- **Form template and Report template.** If you sometimes design forms and/or reports manually (without using a wizard), you can enter the name of an existing form or report to use as a template.

Advanced options

On the Advanced tab (**Figure 20.27**), only two options will be of interest to most new users:

- **Default File Format.** This setting determines whether databases you create can be opened by Access 2000 users or only by 2002/2003 users. The default setting is Access 2000. If you don't intend to share your databases with others or if they all have a current version of Access, you can select Access 2002-2003.

- **Default open mode.** This setting determines the mode Access uses when opening databases: *Shared* (multi-user) or *Exclusive* (single user). If you're on a network and work with shared databases, choose Shared. If you're in a single-user environment or don't share databases, choose Exclusive.

✔ Tip

- Whenever you need to switch between Shared and Exclusive mode, you must make the change on the Advanced tab of the Options dialog box.

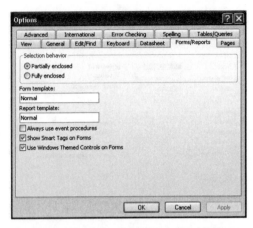

Figure 20.26 The Forms/Reports tab of the Options dialog box.

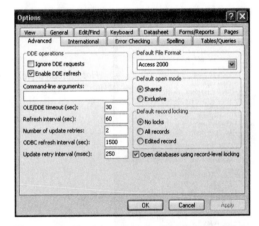

Figure 20.27 The Advanced tab of the Options dialog box.

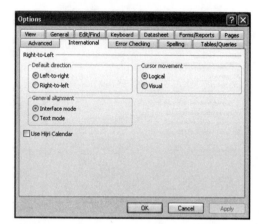

Figure 20.28 The International tab of the Options dialog box.

International options

The options on the International tab (**Figure 20.28**) are of interest only to users who work with databases in Arabic or other right-to-left languages.

◆ **Default direction.** New objects are placed to accommodate users with left-to-right or right-to-left languages.

◆ **Cursor movement.** This setting is only relevant to databases with fields that contain mixed-language text (Arabic and English in the same sentence, for example). If Logical is selected and the cursor is in a mixed-language sentence, it will move from right-to-left through Arabic text and left-to-right through English text. The Visual selection results in a constant movement in one direction when the cursor is in a mixed-language sentence.

◆ **General alignment.** Select Interface mode to set the General alignment setting to be consistent with the language in use. Select Text mode to set the General alignment setting to be consistent with the first language-specific character encountered. (The latter setting is useful for databases that contain text in multiple languages.)

Spelling options

The options on the Spelling tab (**Figure 20.29**) enable you to set a language for the main dictionary, select the custom dictionary to which new words will be added, and specify some general spell-checking rules.

◆ **Dictionary Language.** Select a language for the main spelling dictionary.

◆ **Add words to.** When you click the Add button during a spelling check, the new word is added to the selected custom dictionary. If you have multiple custom dictionaries, you can select a specific one.

◆ **Suggest from main dictionary only.** If this option is checked and an unknown word is flagged during a spelling check, possible replacement words are drawn exclusively from the main dictionary (ignoring the current custom dictionary).

◆ **Ignore.** Ignore options with checkmarks are skipped over during a spelling check. If you occasionally make a certain type of typo (such as hitting a number key in the middle of a word), you can disable the appropriate option(s).

Click the AutoCorrect Options button to view or change settings for AutoCorrect (**Figure 20.30**), the Office tool that fixes common typing errors as you work. While AutoCorrect is considerably more useful in Word, it can be helpful in Access, too.

◆ **Correct/Capitalize.** Set these check boxes to match the way that you work.

◆ **Replace text as you type.** This check box is related to the Replace/With list below it. When enabled, AutoCorrect corrects typos found in the list as you type. To add a new text string and its replacement to the list, enter a frequently mistyped word or phrase in the Replace text box and its replacement in the With text box.

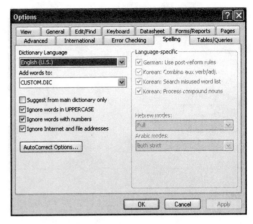

Figure 20.29 The Spelling tab of the Options dialog box.

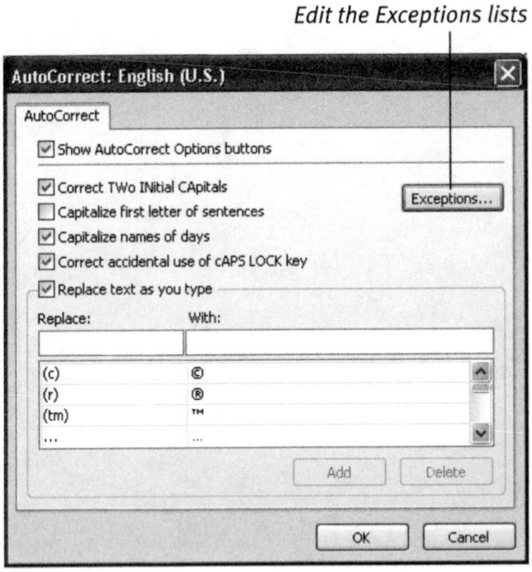

Edit the Exceptions lists

Figure 20.30 AutoCorrect helps you avoid typing errors. It can be very useful if your database has Memo fields, for example.

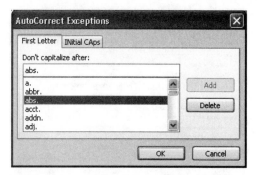

Figure 20.31 The First Letter tab already contains an extensive list of abbreviations that should not be treated as marking the end of a sentence.

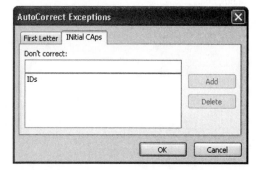

Figure 20.32 The Initial Caps tab, on the other hand, is empty. It's up to you to add the words you use that begin with a pair of capital letters (such as IDs).

◆ **Exceptions.** Click the Exceptions button to view or modify the AutoCorrect Exceptions lists.

▲ *First Letter.* The First Letter tab (**Figure 20.31**) lists abbreviations that should not be treated as the end of a sentence (in order to prevent the first letter of the following word from being inappropriately capitalized).

▲ *Initial Caps.* The Initial Caps tab (**Figure 20.32**) contains the list of words for which the first two letters should properly be capitalized (and, hence, left unchanged by AutoCorrect).

Tables/Queries options

The options on the Tables/Queries tab (**Figure 20.33**) are used to specify design preferences for tables and queries.

The following Table Design options allow you to set new defaults that will be used whenever you create a new table or add fields to an existing table:

◆ **Text.** Specify the default size (in characters) for new Text fields. (Unless you regularly create large non-Memo text fields, you may find that 50 characters is excessive.)

◆ **Number.** Select a default format for Number fields.

◆ **Default field type.** If Text isn't the type of field you create most frequently, select a different one from the drop-down list.

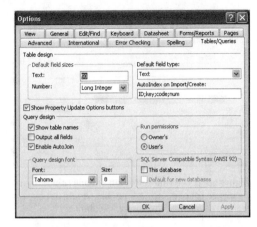

Figure 20.33 The Tables/Queries tab of the Options dialog box.

INDEX

INDEX